CRICUT DESIGN SPACE

vol. 1

THE PERFECT GUIDE TO GET STARTED DESIGNING ON
CRICUT DESIGN SPACE

Made with love

by

Sienna

Tally

TABLE OF CONTENTS

Introduction

Cricut is a machine that helps you in making designs and creating innumerable arts and crafts projects. It is such a hit among enthusiasts because it works on paper and can also create and cut designs for other materials like vinyl, cloth, cardboard, and more. You can even use it for wood!

Professional designers and artists mostly use it for their different projects. However, Cricut is becoming a household name through the sleek design's availability, where even young people can experiment to check their creative strengths. Through a Cricut machine, you can draw, emboss or deboss and then cut out your chosen design.

The best thing about this fantastic piece of technology is that its usage is pretty simple. It means that even if you have never used such a device before, or if you are new to the world of art, you can still learn to use the Cricut machine with some guidance.

And this is why Cricut Design Space is ideal. It helps users develop ideas, styles, drawings, and more to generate something unique and distinctly their own.

Cricut for Business

Have you been thinking of working from home and set up your own business? Have you always been into arts and crafts, clothing, or woodwork? Then Cricut machine can help you establish your very own business right from the comfort of your house. Through the use of Cricut Design Space, you can come up with beautiful, original designs that can then be used to start up your own business. Depending on what you wish to do, you can have your woodwork place, your boutique with cutwork clothes, and even an arts-and-crafts, Etsy-type store.

Your Cricut Design Space app will help you select designs that are already available and customize them to come up with something different that isn't already present in the market. It would become a kind of signature style that only your business promotes and sells.

Not sure how this can work out? Let's consider an example. So, you are into quilt designs. You have already worked on some, and everyone around you loves to have you gift them something. You know you have a talent but don't have the stamina or the strength to keep creating quilts after quilts. Meet your best friend, the

Cricut machine that will make quilting a unique yet enjoyable experience for you. With a Cricut Maker's help, you can easily cut all shapes while using hundreds of fabrics. The accuracy and precision that you will obtain through this machine are going to throw you in awe. And the best part? Your work will be done at least in a triple faster time. You will not have to spend weeks on one quilt because your Cricut machine will get the job done in a few short days! If once you were only able to quilt one quilt a month, you will now create many. Just imagine the business you will have. Your passion will be making money for you!

And then once you have begun, there is no stopping you. With the help of social media, you can popularize your business venture in a short period and quickly make a name for yourself in the world of quiltmakers.

Of course, how big or small you wish to keep your business will be up to you. In some time, you may even be able to hire help to do extra work for you! Enticed? Think about it even more and remember, quilting is only one such business that your Cricut machine will help you start. There are many other options that you can choose from.

The only thing you will need to put your mind to is what you like doing and whether or not that venture will have any demand in your area. The whole point of a small-scale business or home-based business is that you pick a project you know is in order. So, get researching and find out what you can do with your skillful and innovative Cricut machine and your Cricut Design Space.

The Many Projects You Can Start with Cricut

A Cricut machine cuts stuff for you in all the shapes, sizes, and varieties you can think of. It means it is a crafter's dream come true, no matter what industry they belong to. If you are one such crafter, then here are all the things you can do with a Cricut machine.

1.   Creating Cards

One of the most straightforward and essential things you can do with a Cricut machine is creating cards. You can cut out any shape of any size and either stick it on cards or even cut your card design in a specific manner. With the help of your Cricut Design Space, you can cut and flip shapes to create a unique design and weld together different formats into one whole. You can even align lines to precision, arrange various elements to see how they would go together, rotate shapes to fit them correctly and try different fonts and sizes. Most importantly, you can attach all the things to cut in just the right manner.

Depending on what kind of cards you want to create, you can decide the color combination and the shape. The machine and Cricut Design Space app's whole point is to explore as many options as you can think of. The app allows you to visualize what you would otherwise only have had in your head.

2.   Vinyl Projects

Vinyl is another thing that you can use for your Cricut projects. Vinyl is a kind of plastic used for multiple items, from food labels to crayon holders, stencils, and more. With the aid of a Cricut machine, you can easily create various designs for pretty much everything you can think of. But what is even better is that the Design Space app will help you believe first out through virtual design to figure out if it is even possible to come up with a product that you have imagined in your head. Be it shapes, sizes, or cuts, you can either choose them from the samples given, or you can come up with your signature style.

Of course, you will have to find out which type of vinyl is best for what kind of product. So do your research before beginning any project.

3.   Home Décor

Just the thought of home décor sends some people into rapturous reviews, while others would only groan at the idea. If you fall into the former category, then Cricut is your new best buddy. Why? Because you can design multiple objects with this machine and its perfect app. From spice baskets to children's toys, wall art, to hanging plant holders, you think it, and the device can do it for you. You can even come up with unique designs that are distinctly your own. People would be mesmerized by what you can do with your imagination.

These DIY home décor items will be projects to opt for all the rooms in your house and outside the house. You can easily create your door wreaths, planters, even fake plants if that is what you wish!

The great thing about these DIY projects is that they are one of a kind that no one else can make. You can even make gifts for your loved ones or the dear ones who love personalized presents. Imagine how people will love the effort you put in, giving them something to remember you by.

4.   Jewelry

It's another thing that you can do with Cricut. Jewelry making is a fine art, and not everyone had the talent to come up with beautiful designs. With Cricut design space, you can bring to screen what you have in your mind's eye.

The perfect thing about using Cricut is that you can engage the entire family in this process. If your young ones have an interest in creative projects, then this is something they will enjoy immensely. Since a Cricut machine can be used for various materials, you can easily make artificial jewelry with it.

You can opt for different materials like wood, plastic, rubber, stone, gemstone, resin, and even vinyl for your jewelry projects. Just make sure that you do not allow very young children to handle it when it comes to the machine's actual usage. Even older kids will need some guidance from you. But as far as the use of design space is concerned, everyone who understands it can use it without supervision. Jewelry making was never as simple as it is with a Cricut machine.

5.   Woodwork

It is another handy creative work that you can enjoy alone, with family or even friends. The best part is that you cannot just make things with wood for your pleasure but also sell it and establish your venture. Keep in mind that a Cricut maker can cut materials that are less than 2.4 mm thick. It would help if you also had a new knife blade that is sharper and thicker for wood cutting, and you would have to purchase it separately.

When it comes to the type of woods for Cricut maker, basswood and balsa wood are ideal because they have a smooth texture that is easy to cut. What's more, the finishing that you can obtain with these woods is incomparable to any other. This is why most people who use Cricut maker for woodwork opt for these types of wood.

One more tip for woodwork is to make sure that you mark the wood with tapes while cutting to don't end up with wood with irregular cuttings. You can make frames, figurines, jewelry, ornaments, and even puzzle toys for kids! Design Space helps you make sure that all the pieces are perfectly aligned to one another by giving you the precision of design and cut.

6.   Holiday Items

Once you have a Cricut Maker, you can pretty much stop buying gifts from shops because you now can make them on your own. You can make your cards or personalized gifts like quilts, jewelry, décor items, and even acrylic items for birthdays. If you want to make it even more personal, create a kind of gift with their vinyl name on it! Imagine the look of pleasure when you present your mom or dad, for example, with a birthday rug that says "best Mom/Dad" that you made yourself! They will be over the moon!

But birthdays aren't the only occasions that can be blessed with your Cricut machine. You can make Christmas gifts, Easter eggs/surprises, Halloween decorations, as well as costumes with your Cricut machine. Did you know that you can even carve your pumpkin with a Cricut machine? Yes, life does become more fun when introducing the Cricut machine and Design Space to your family and friends.

And that's not it; you can even make your holiday decoration items, like ornaments, for Christmas. From the angel at the top to Halloween toppers for your food corner, you can pretty much come up with any holiday decoration. You can go as far as your imagination can take you.

There is so much that you can do without having to spend hundreds of dollars during the holiday season!

7.   Clothing

Clothing is another thing that the Cricut machine and Design Space can be used for. There are so many sample options that you can choose from, mix and match them, and come up with your unique style. From ordinary day clothes, special occasion costumes, to clothes for your loved ones, you can make whatever you envision.

But clothes aren't the only thing you can create. Anything made of fabric can easily be cut with a Cricut machine or designed on the Design app. Pillow cushions, throw rugs, curtains, doilies, rugs, blankets, quilts, you can decorate and create anything that you want. Sky seriously is the limit when it comes to the Cricut machine. Want to do patchwork? Cricut is there to save you hours of the day by cutting up patches in any size, all the same, as frequently, and as quickly as you want.

If you like sewing and making your clothes, you can also present them to your loved ones. If not, you can always customize blank tees, jackets, and jeans with your Cricut design space.

Customizing clothing and fabric had never been more comfortable.

8.   3-D Projects

Ever been fascinated by the idea of 3-D projects? If you have the circuit machine and Design Space, then it is something that you can try for yourself. You can make your paper toys, gift boxes, and your wood items, as mentioned above.

Cricut is also ideal for professional architects and designers because they understand the need for and importance of 3-D designs. You can quickly draw on the screen what you wish to make and then bring it to reality through your Cricut machine. The best part? Unlike doing things with hands, it will not take you ages; you can do it within a few short minutes. What's more, the results are going to be precise like you may never have envisioned before. Now that you know about the actual machine, what it can do, and who it is best suited for, let's now figure out how you can take maximum benefit from it through the application of Cricut Design Space.

Chapter 1
What Cricut Machines are Compatible with Cricut Design Space

WHAT IS THE CRICUT DESIGN SPACE?

The Cricut design space is the web-based program considered to be the backbone of the Cricut machine. You get to access the thousands of predefined projects (templates) that you can customize to create your personalized designs or start creating yours from scratch on this application. This platform holds about 75,000 images, more than 800 predesigned templates, and about 400 fonts, giving you a vast array of options to choose from when creating your projects or customizing any of the pre-created projects you will come across the platform.

In a nutshell, the Cricut design space is simply where the magic of designing happens, and access to this platform is the reason why you need to sign up with an internet-connected device in the first place.

You can do other things in this space, including uploading your jpeg and SVG images, customizing your fonts to suit your needs, and generally unleash the creative genius in you.

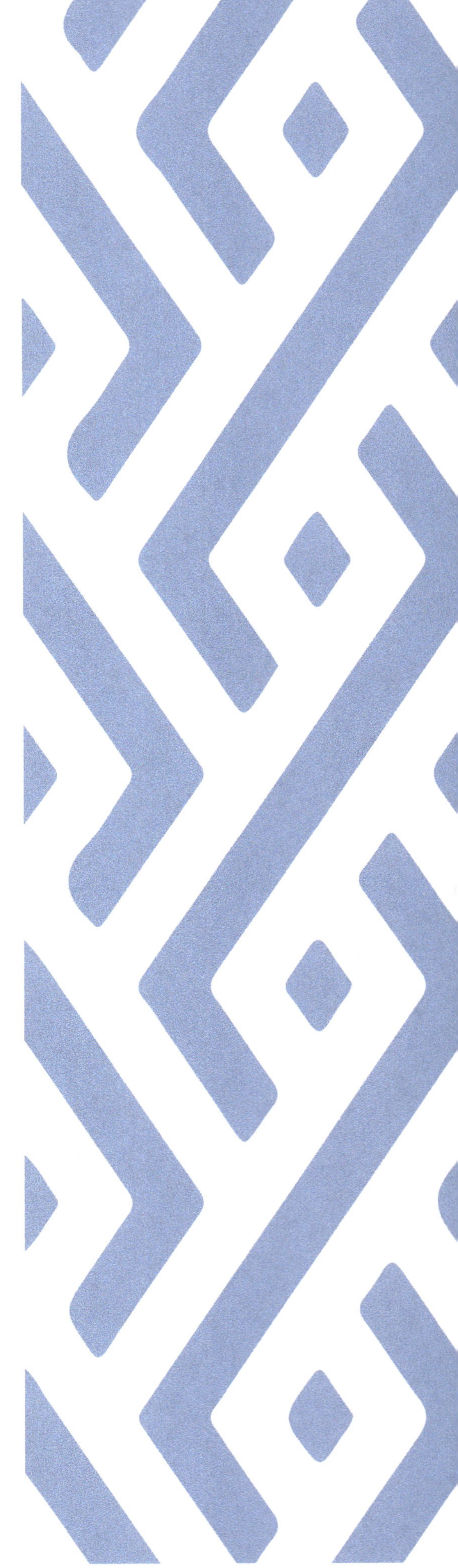

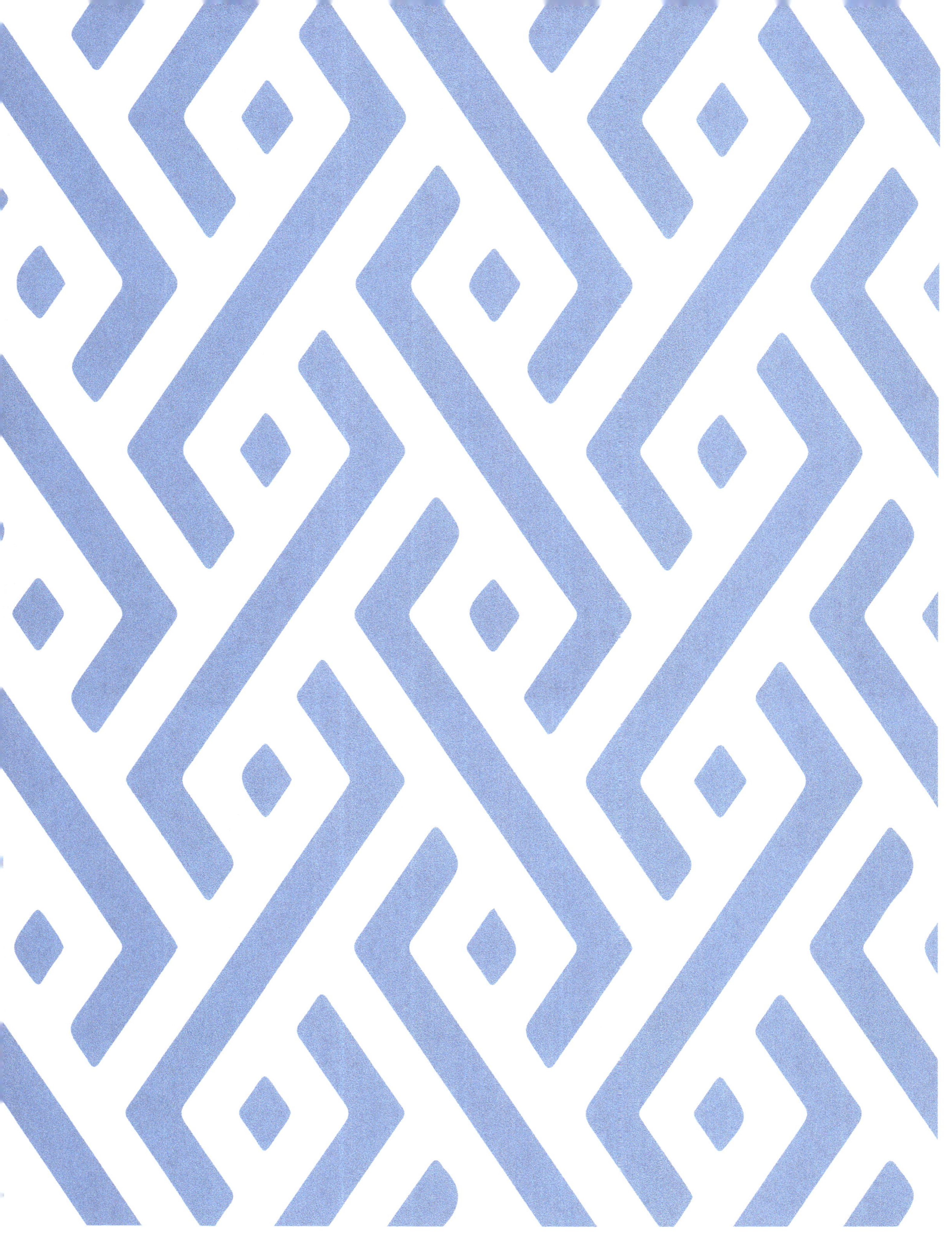

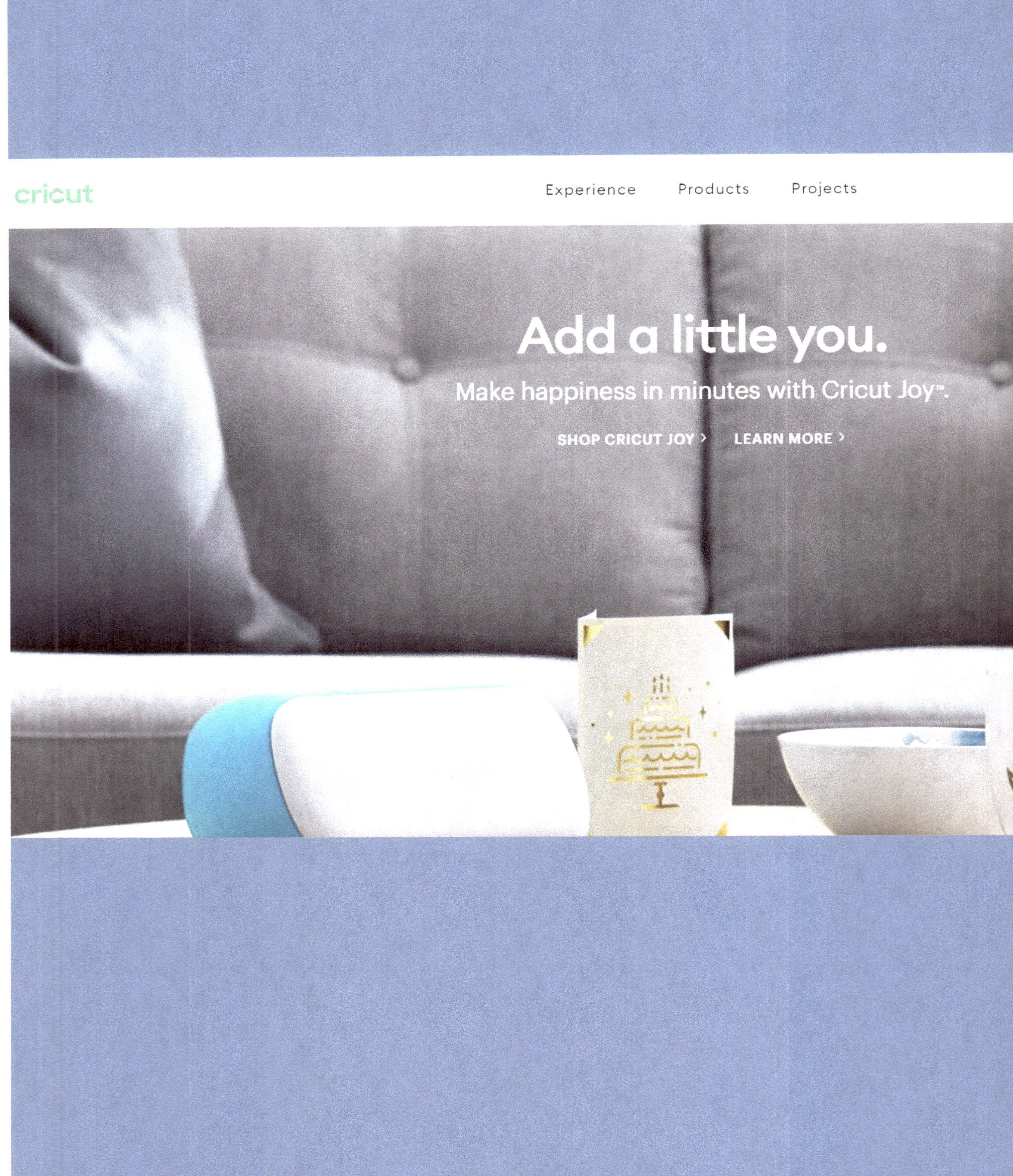

cricut
Experience   Products   Projects
Add a little you.
Make happiness in minutes with Cricut Joy™.
SHOP CRICUT JOY >   LEARN MORE >

WHICH CRICUT MACHINES ARE COMPATIBLE WITH DESIGN SPACE?

All the motorized cutting machines they have on the market are compatible. It includes the Cricut Explore, Cricut Explore Air, Cricut Explore Air 2, and the Cricut Maker. With the current Design Space version, you can use all of these tools to build countless projects for each style.

HOW DOES THE DESIGN SPACE WORK?

It is not just enough to know that the CDS is an essential tool; you must know how it works. Navigating your way through the CDS can be a bit overwhelming, especially if you are new to the use of this space and the Cricut. This is because of the many functionalities that are found in the space. If you are not trained to make use of these functionalities and to know what each of them stands for, you may not be able to make use of the platform, and you will see that you will be at a loss for what to do every time you are about to create your designs or launch a project. We will take a deep dive into the CDS and help you better understand what it is all about and how you can find your way around it.

Creating your projects and everything you want to cut out with your machine is done on a window called the canvas. Consider your canvas to be where you get to carry out all the designs you will carry out. Like the artist's painting canvas is where all the magic happens, your design space canvas is where you get to create and work on every project you have to work on. Attached to your canvas are many buttons and icons that can create in you that sense of despair or the feeling that navigating the design space will be an arduous task. The truth is, once you can look over that claustrophobic feeling you get by looking at all the icons on the canvas, you will discover that the design space is not as difficult to use as it appears.

When you log into your design space, you will be taken to the application's home screen. On the home screen, you will see a lot of thumbnail pictures. These are templates that you can customize to create your projects, and as a beginner, you may want to start by trying out this step. It may be difficult to start creating your designs from scratch, so the best move sometimes may be to start by customizing a template to suit your needs.

You can, however, start a new project if you feel that you have what it takes to do so immediately. When starting on a project, you will notice that the canvas has many grids. Grids are the thin lines that separate the entire canvas into small boxes. While these may seem as though they are not of any use to you, this is not the case because these grids play a significant role in making sure that you create the best possible project. Grids help you visualize the cutting mat and keeps your work together as they serve as tools for calibration. With them, you end up maximizing your design space and achieving the best you can. Grids are calibrated in inches and cm. You can toggle these calibration units, depending on what you are looking to achieve and the calibrations you have at hand. Toggling is a straightforward process; all you need to do is click on the top panel and adjust the desired settings.

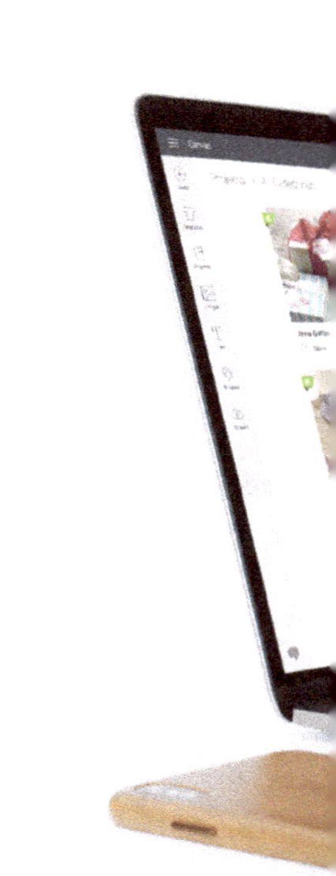

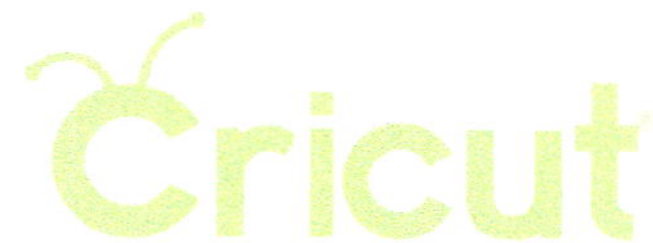

Design Space® for Mac

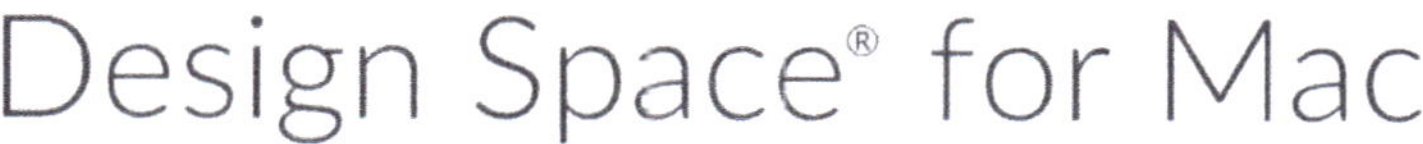

Take me to the old Design Space for Web. I'll upgrade later.

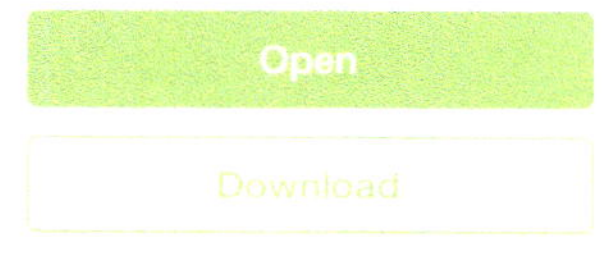

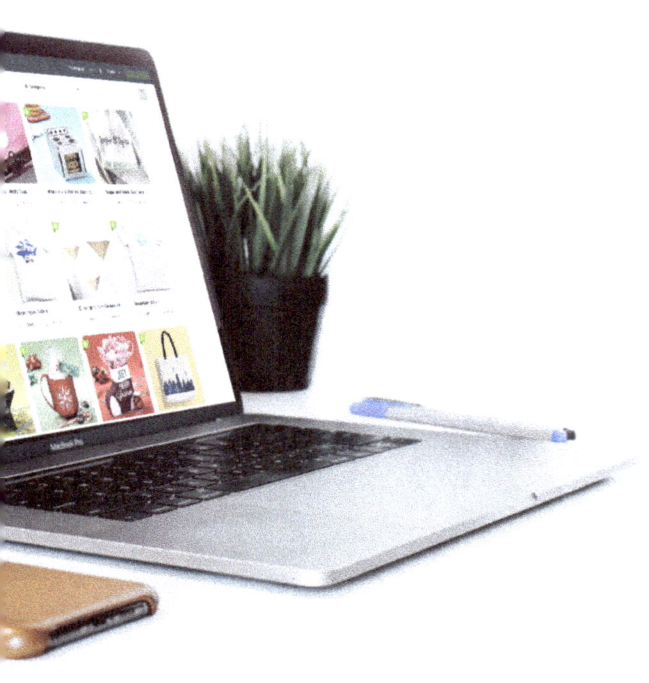

With your design space and all the tools there, you can create projects from scratch, import some features from an external point, and customize the projects that pop up on your home screen after logging into the design space application. A lot can be achieved using the application, and you always need to remember that this is where all the magic happens, as far as designing projects are concerned.

This is what the design space home screen and the working canvas look like, respectively.

Canvas
Unti
New
Templates
Projects
Images
Text
Shapes
Upload
0
1
2
3
4
5
6
7
8
9
0
1
2
3
4
5

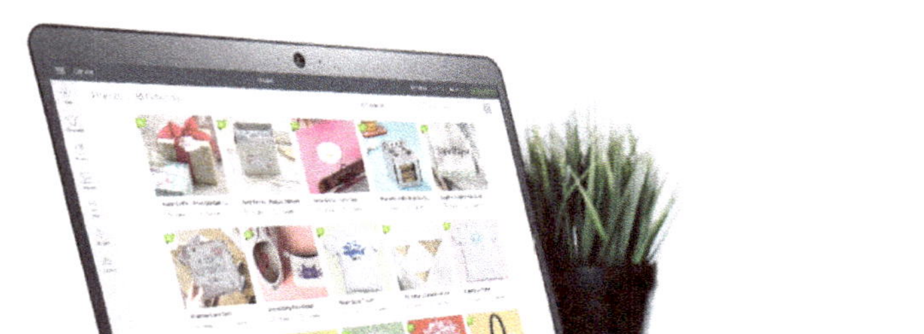

cricut
Downloading Design Space® f
Set up a new Cricut product, browse projects, start designing, and mor
In your Downloads folder, double click the file named Cricut Design Spa
Having trouble?
Cricut Design Spac....exe

Chapter 2
Downloading and Installing Design Space

HOW TO INSTALL/UNINSTALL DESIGN SPACE

Different platforms use Cricut Design Space. Let us learn how to install/uninstall on these platforms, including Windows, Mac, iOS, and Android devices. Install on Windows/Mac:

- Click on your browser and navigate to www.design.cricut.com
- If you are a first-time user, you need to create a Cricut ID; otherwise, sign in with your Cricut ID. Ensure that the page is fully loaded before carrying out this activity to avoid an error.
- Select New Project.
- Select Download Plugin from the prompt.
- Wait for the download to finish and then select the downloaded file to Open/Run it.
- Click Next when the Cricut installer opens.
- Read the Terms of Use and accept the agreement.
- Click Install to begin the installation
- Click Done at the end of the installation.

INSTALL CRICUT DESIGN SPACE APP ON IOS

- Tap on the App Store icon on your device

- Search for Cricut Design Space
- Tap the Get button to download. Please confirm the download with your iTunes password if prompted. The app will launch and display the necessary options that will be used to complete the process.

INSTALL CRICUT DESIGN SPACE APP ON ANDROID

- Tap Google Play Store App on your device to open it
- Search for Cricut Design Space
- Tap on the Install button
- Tap on the Cricut Design Space icon to open it when the installation is complete
- Sign in and start designing your project

UNINSTALL THE CRICUT DESIGN SPACE ON IOS

- Press and hold the Design Space icon on your iOS device till it vibrates
- Press the X button to delete it from your device. This is very easy, right?
- Uninstall Cricut Design Space App on Android
- Go to Settings
- Tap on "Apps" or "Applications"
- Swipe to the "Download" tab or "Application Manager."
- Search for the App you intend to uninstall
- Tap the "Uninstall" button to finish, and the App is gone for good.

UNINSTALL ON MAC

cricut design space
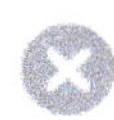

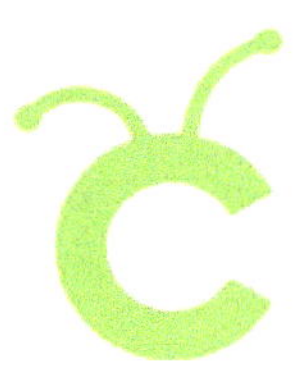

Cricut Design Space
Provo Craft & Novelty
★ ★ ★ ★ ☆ (137)

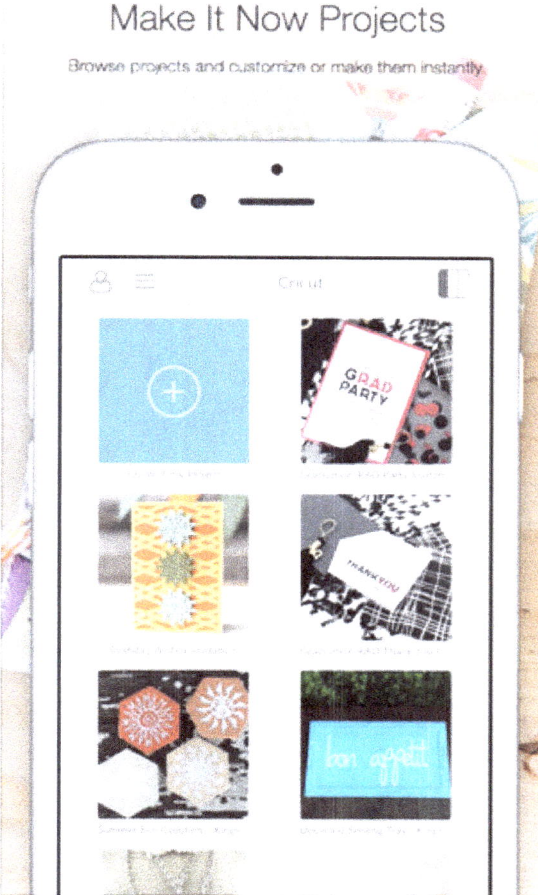
Make It Now Projects
Browse projects and customize or make them instantly.

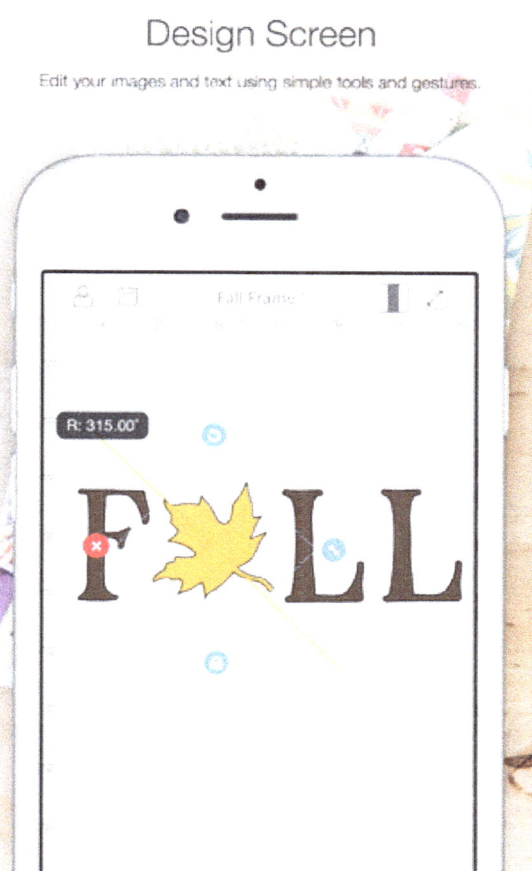
Design Screen
Edit your images and text using simple tools and gestures.
R: 315.00°
F LL

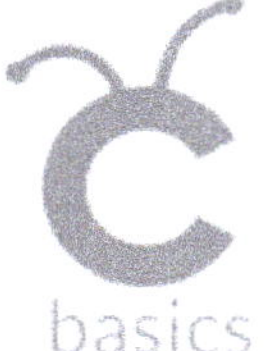

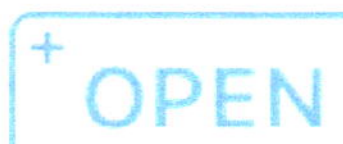

Cricut Basics
Provo Craft & Novelty
★ ★ ★ ★ ★ (8)
OPEN

STEP 1   STEP 2

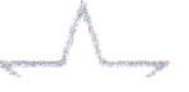
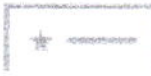
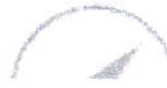

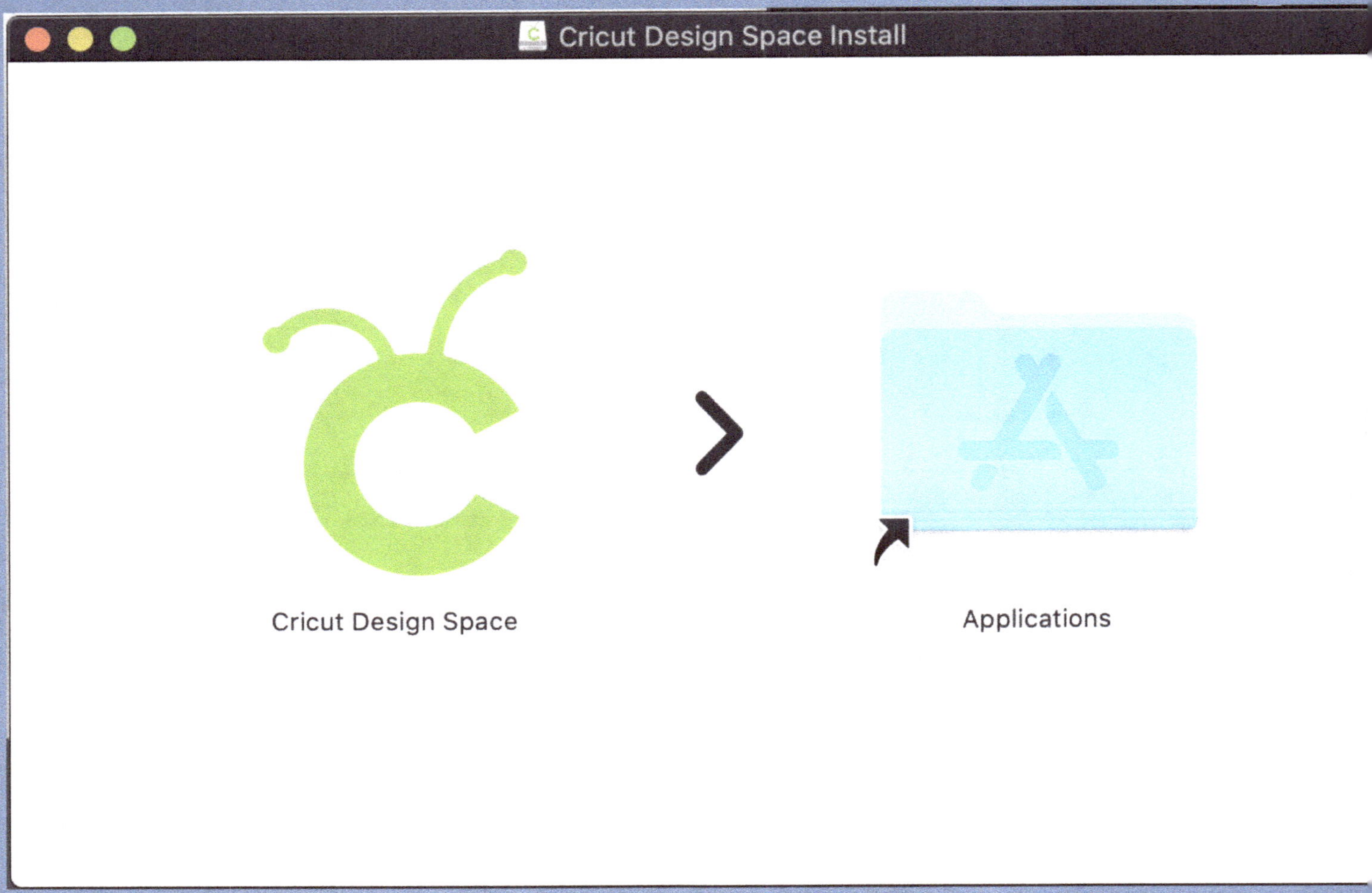

Cricut Design Space Install

Cricut Design Space

Applications

- Move to Finder and oper the Applications folder
- Search for Cricut Design Space
- Drag it to trash
- Right-click on the Trashcan anc select Empty Trash to remove the Application

UNINSTALL ON WINDOWS

- Click on the Start button.
- Select Settings
- Select Application
- Look for Cricut Design Space and choose Uninstall

HOW TO CENTER YOUR DESIGNS TO CUT IN CRICUT DESIGN SPACE?

- Sign in to the Cricut Design section. Click on the new project.
- Click Download.
- Click Upload Picture.
- Click Browse.
- Save your picture
- Select the saved image and insert an image.
- Select the picture. Click or it.
- As you can see, the picture is automatically moved to the upper left corner.
- To prevent this, you can fool the software by placing the image in the center of your design area and the mat. This is useful if you want to create openings in the middle of a page.
- Click on the shape tool.
- Create a shape of 11.5 x 11.5 inches.
- Select the square and change the setting to cut

it in the drawing.

- The square now appears as an outline.
- Click Align and Center with the selected pattern and square.
- Click the arrow of your square's size and resize it without moving the top left corner to reduce the square's size.
- Select the square and pattern, then click Attach. Click on it.
- As you can see now, the design is centered.

HOW TO WRITE WITH SKETCH PENS IN CRICUT DESIGN SPACE

- Sign in to the Cricut Design section. Create a new project.
- Click Download.
- Select upload a picture.
- Click Browse.
- Open your file. Then save. To get a good effect, use a file with thin lines and no large spaces.
- Click on the pattern and paste it.
- Select the pattern.
- Change the drawing to a drawing.
- You will now see the drawing as an outline drawn.
- Click on it.
- Your drawing will now be displayed on the cutting screen. Click on Continue.
- If you change your drawing to draw, the software automatically selects the pen tool. Insert the pen or marker into the recommended clip. Insert paper and click on the start icon.
- The pen now draws your pattern.

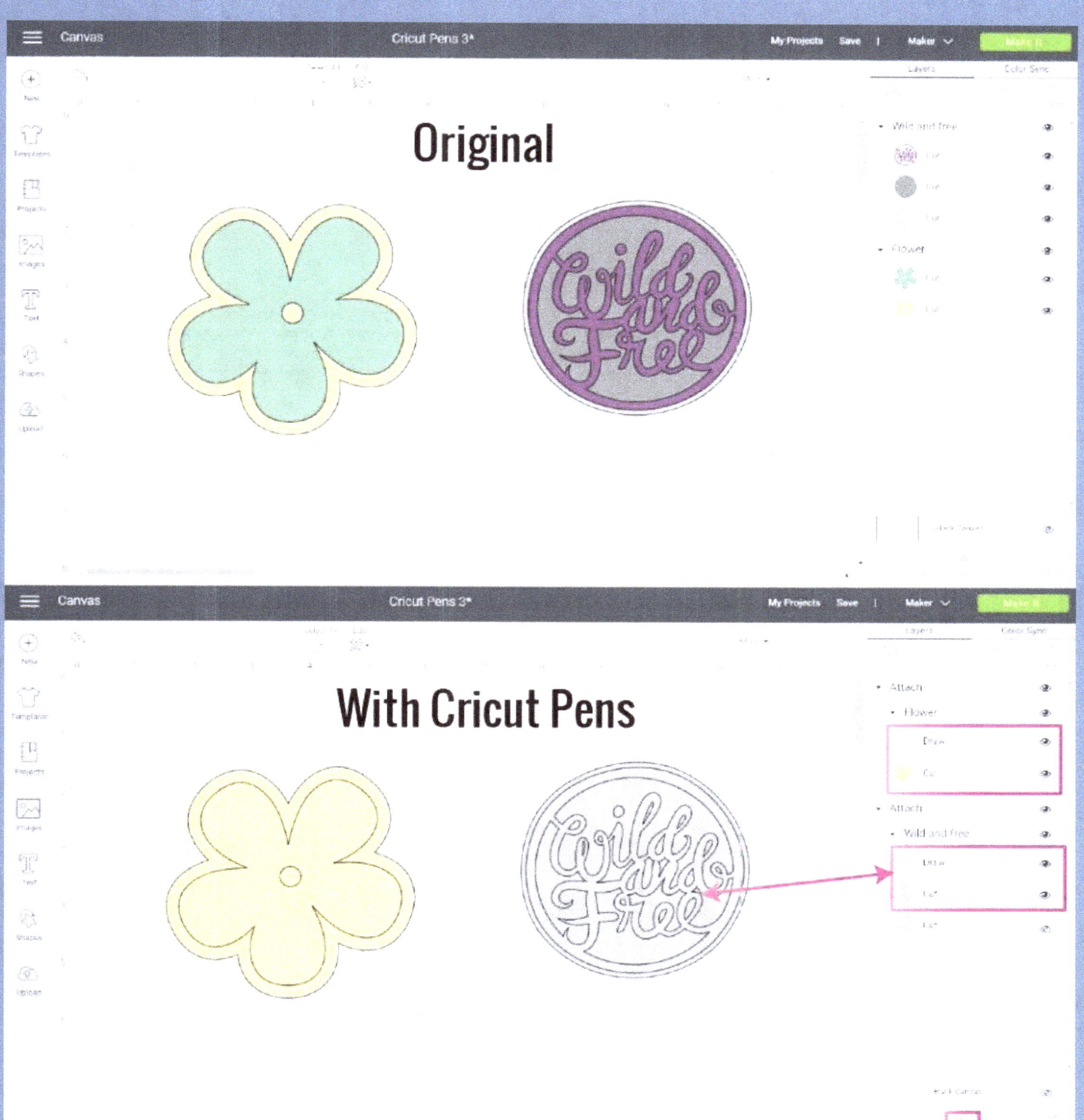
Original
With Cricut Pens
Wild and free

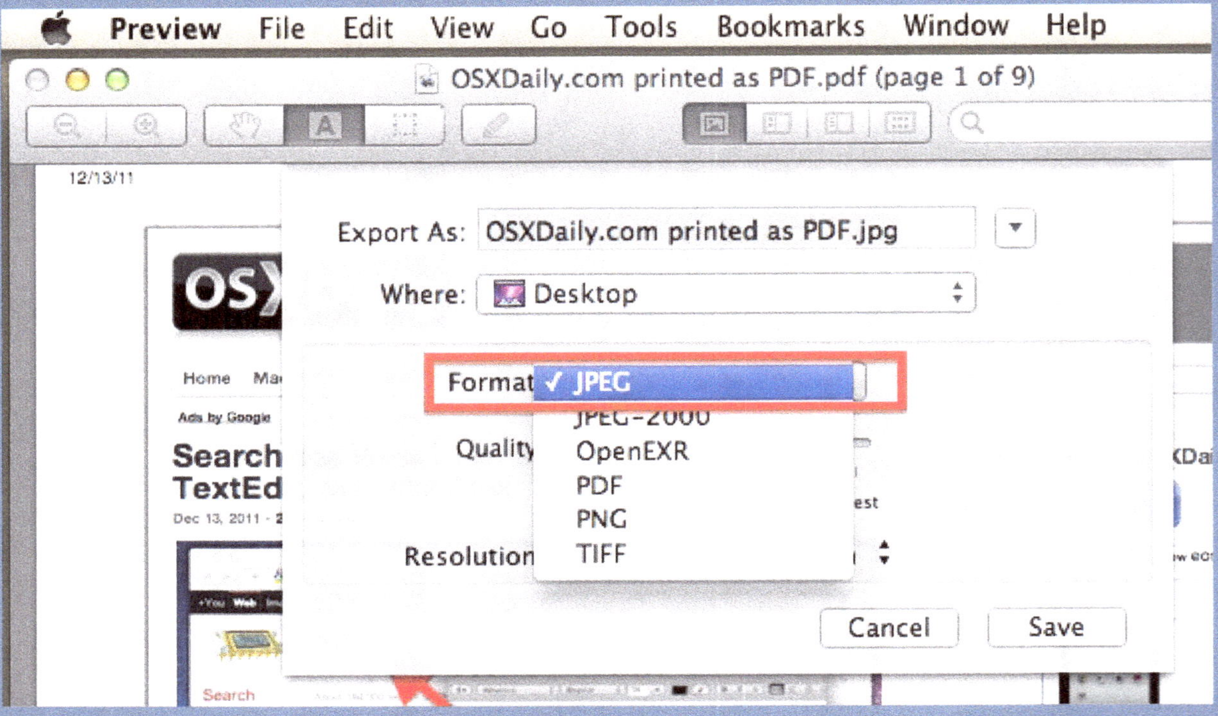

Preview   File   Edit   View   Go   Tools   Bookmarks   Window   Help
OSXDaily.com printed as PDF.pdf (page 1 of 9)
12/13/11
Export As: OSXDaily.com printed as PDF.jpg
Where: Desktop
Format √ JPEG
JPEG-2000
Quality
OpenEXR
PDF
PNG
Resolution
TIFF
Cancel   Save

HOW TO UPLOAD PNG FILE IN CRICUT DESIGN SPACE?

After you've converted your PDF document to PNG file format, there are some ways to clean up the file before printing and then crop it with Cricut® Design Space.

- Click Create New Project.
- Click Upload Picture.
- Click on the image to upload
- Click Browse
- The Open dialog box opens. Select the PNG file you want to upload and click
- An example of a picture can be found in Cricut® Design Space. Since we want to edit this file, we select Complex Image and click Next
- The PNG file is loaded into Cricut® Design Space. Select and Delete

HOW TO CONVERT A–PDF TO PNG FORMAT?

After downloading the PDF document to your computer, open your browser and go to png2pdf.com.
· Click on the upload files
· The "Open File" dialog box starts. Locate the PDF file to convert (probably in the Downloads folder), click the PDF file and click the file is uploaded. You should see a progress bar. Once the file has been uploaded and converted, a Download button appears below the uploaded file's small image.
· Click on the download. The file is downloaded as a ZIP file and appears in the status bar at the bottom of the screen. Just click on the filename to open the ZIP file.

· The Open File dialog opens, and the downloaded file should be displayed. Since the file is still in ZIP format, you must first unzip or unzip it. Just click Extract All Files.

· The Open File dialog opens, and your newly converted PDF file should be displayed in a PNG file. You can open the file with a double-click if you only want to see what the file looks like. Close the window now by clicking on the red X.

· After you have converted your PDF file to PNG format, you must upload the PNG file to Cricut® Design Space so that you can use the Print and Cut functions.

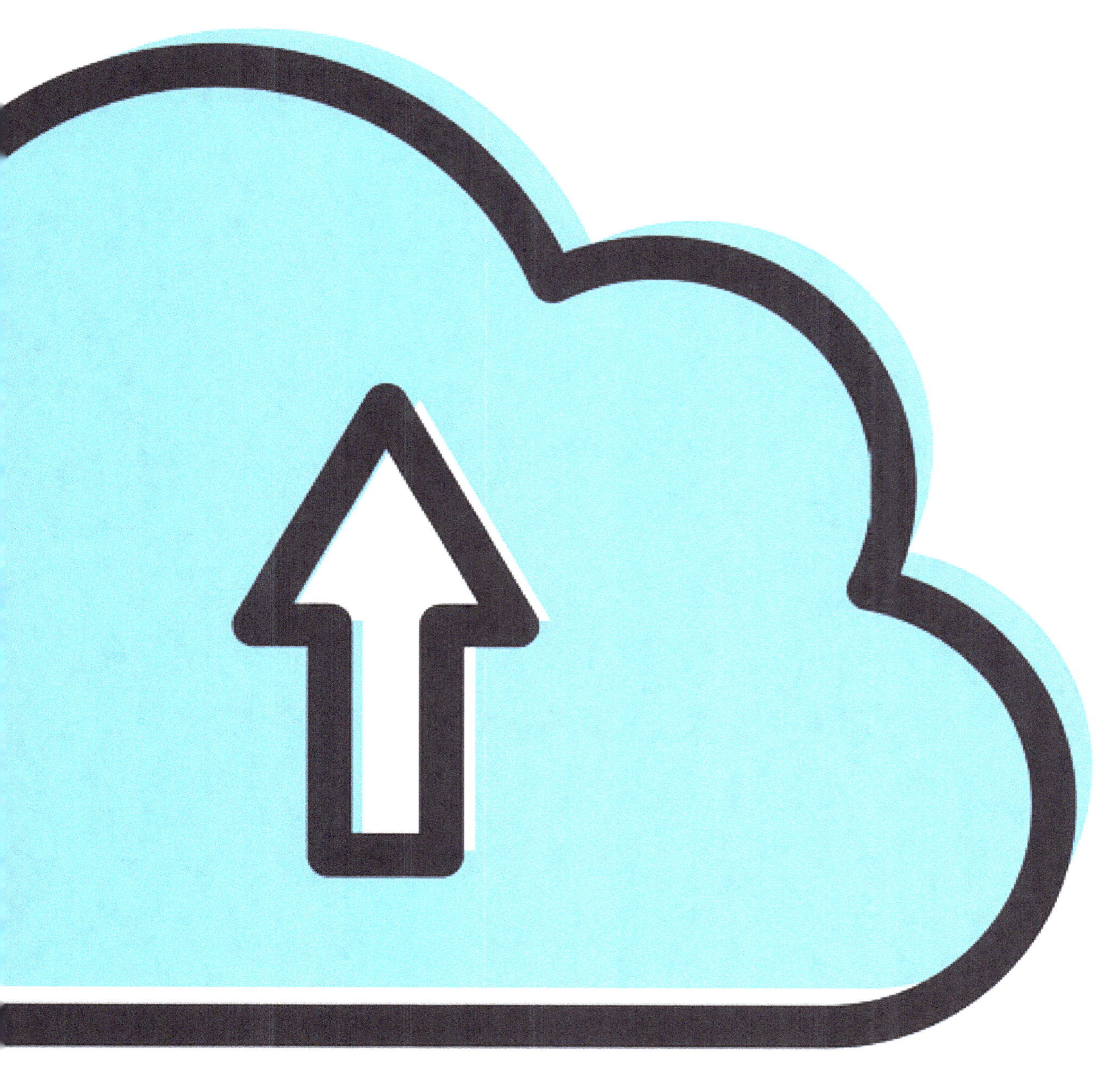

a

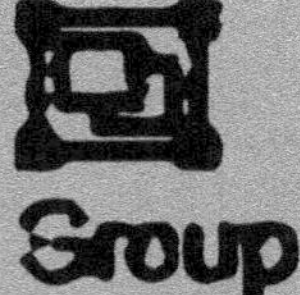

Group

UnGroup

Duplicate

Delete

Chapter 3
Design Space App

As a Cricut user, knowing the necessary tools and functions of the Cricut Design Space is essential. Not knowing them means you can't handle even the simplest of projects on your own, which doesn't look too good. To ensure you have the right foundation, a foundation that can build you to attain mastery, here we will take you through all the fundamental tools and functions of the Cricut Design Space. Don't worry about using these tools and functions now; simply ensure that you know how they work. This is all that learning is about; know how things work and making exploits with them.

RUDIMENTARY TOOLS

Tools are essential in every work; you can barely make progress without them. Every field of work has its tools, so does the Design Space. Sometimes, the number of tools you use during your project can determine your project's beauty. There're so many tools in the Design Space, and we shall take a look at most of them and what they are used for.

CRICUT DESIGN SPACE CANVAS AREA

Slice
Weld
Attach
Flatten
Contour

Starting with the Canvas area is that all the arts and designing happen on this platform. The Canvas area is where you'll be making use of your tools the most. You can easily carry out the organizing of your projects and the uploading of fonts and images here.

The Design Space is parallel wth many other designing and editing programs people use out there if you look closely. Programs such as Photoshop, Illustrator, and Adobe Creative Cloud are all similar to Cricut Design Space. Therefore, if you've got prior experience using these programs, you shouldn't find it too challenging to flow with the Cricut Design Space.

The Canvas area is where your designs can be edited and perfected before cutting them. Nonetheless, there're several options to explore when working on the Canvas area, and you might get overwhelmed easily. So, we will be discussing these options one after another, making their uses known as we proceed.

The Canvas area consists of four panes: the right panel, left panel, top panel, and canvas area.

THE RIGHT PANEL

The Right panel is made up of layers; therefore, it's safe to call it the "Layers Panel." Layers indicate the designs present in the Canvas area. The number of layers you'll be using will depend on your project's intricacy of design.

Take a birthday card, for example; you'll have different texts and decorations on it, and possibly one or two pictures. These are called the layers of your design.

This panel enables the creation and management of layers when a design is being made. All the items on the Layer Panel will show the Line type or Fill you're using.

GROUP, UNGROUP, DUPLICATE AND DELETE.

These tools enable the moving around of different designs on the Canvas area.

·   Group: This tool permits you to join or group different layers. When many layers need to come together to form a design, then you can use the "Group" tool to bring everything together. For instance, if you're designing a house or building, there'll be diverse parts and sections in that building. A typical building should have a door, roof, windows, and walls. The Group tool will enable you to organize every layer and ensure that they all stay together whenever making the design.

·   Ungroup: You can likewise detach a design made up of many layers by using the Ungroup tool. It only does the opposite of what "Group" does.

·   Duplicate: This tool is self-explanatory. It merely duplicates whichever layer you choose on the Canvas.

·   Delete: This tool gets rid of the layers you choose. It'll delete it permanently away from the Canvas.

BLACK CANVAS

This layer is located on the Right panel. It enables you to modify the current Canvas color. If you're trying out different looks on your design, this option

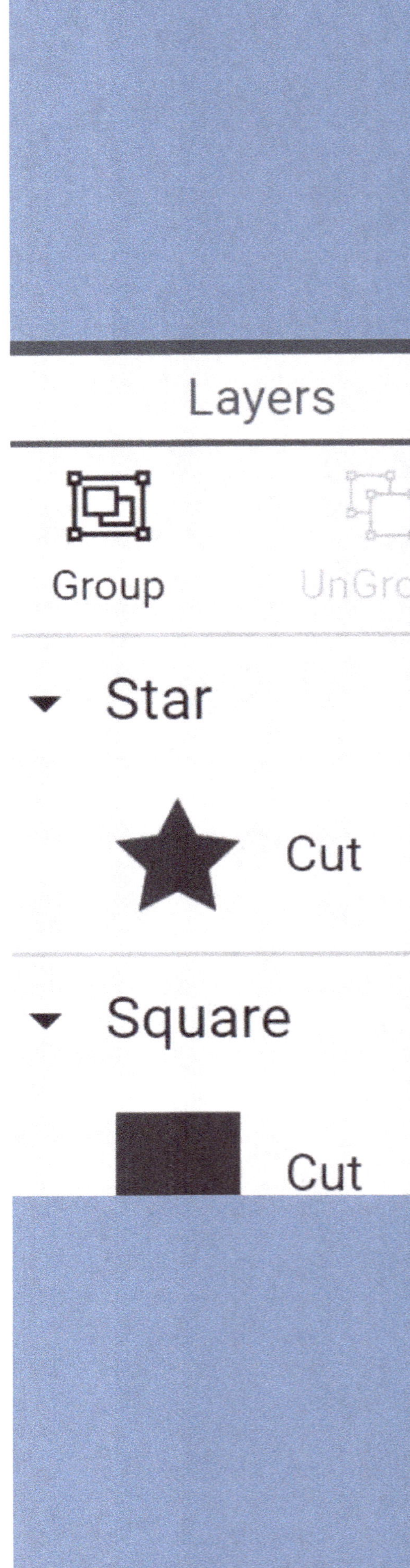

36

Color Sy

Duplicate

can be used to place your design against numerous backgrounds.

LAYER VISIBILITY

This icon in the image above indicates the visibility of your design or layer. You'll find it on all layers on the Panel. It can be used when you're designing, and you observe that a particular element or segment looks odd; you can then click on the icon to get it hidden. Doing that will make sure you don't remove it permanently if you want it back later. Hidden items can be recognized with a visible cross mark.

SLICE, WELD, ATTACH, FLATTEN, AND CONTOUR

It's vital to study how to utilize these five tools maximally. They'll always come in handy, regardless of whatever you're designing.

- Slice: Cricut made this tool for its users to carve out shapes, texts, and diverse elements from an entire design.
- Weld: This is majorly used for merging shapes to form a new one. If you desire to make something different or creative with your design, you can combine different shapes.
- Attach: Attach is more like an advanced version of the "Group" tool. It joins shapes and modifies their colors to fit the background color you're using. These changes will still be in effect even after you're done cutting.
- Flatten: This tool will be handy when you're about printing different shapes. To flatten different

shapes, select the layers you desire to print, and then pick the "Flatten" option.

·   Contour: You can use this option if you desire to hide an entire layer or a small part of a design layer. However, this can only be done when the layers in your design can be separated.

COLOR SYNC

This tool is designed for balancing out your design and background colors. It can likewise be used to change diverse shades of a design color to a single color. As the name implies, Color Sync synchronizes the colors.

LEFT PANEL

The Left Panel consists of every option needed for inserting. Shapes, images, texts, and even ready-to-cut projects can be added. With the Left Panel, you can insert everything you want to cut. The Left Panel has seven options; let's quickly explore them all consecutively.

NEW

This option can be selected when you desire a new page. This new page is different from the page that you're designing with. It's better to save all your current designs before moving on to the page you just created. This is done to keep your designs in case you'll be needing them later. If you don't save before moving tc the page you just created, your initial designs will be lost.

Layers   Color Sync

This panel allows you to sync colors to use fewer materials. To change an object color, drag and drop that object into the layer of the desired color.

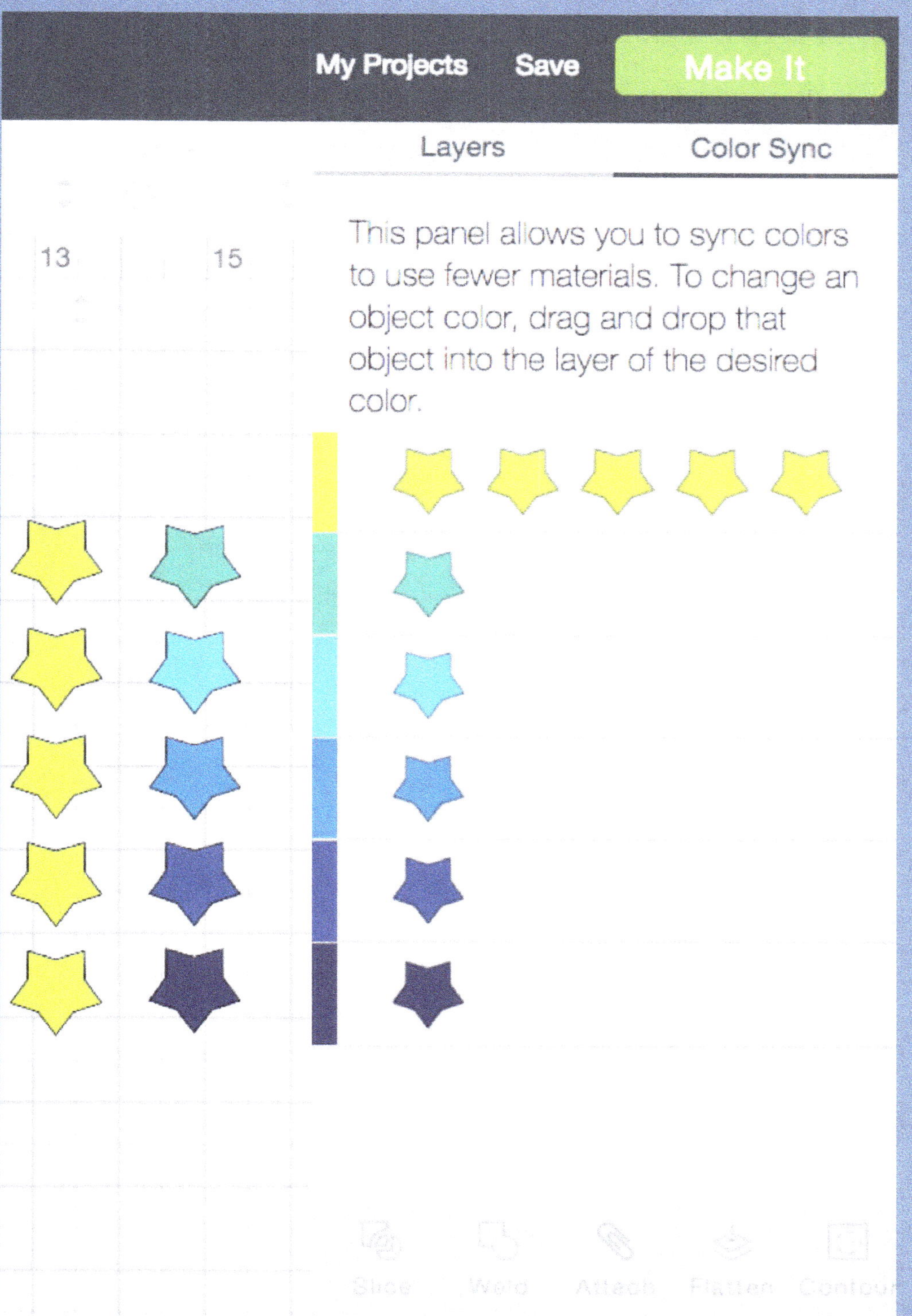

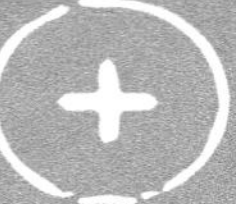
New

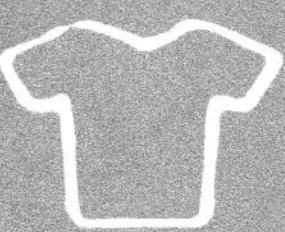
Templates

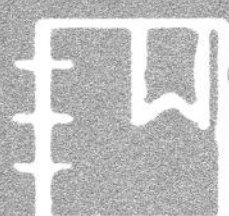
Projects

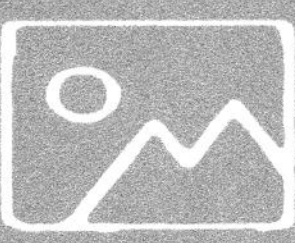
Images

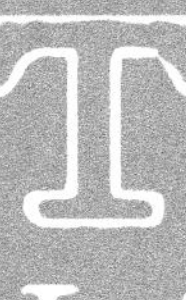
Text

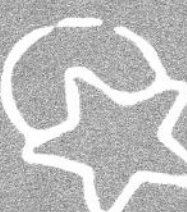
Shapes

Upload

TEMPLATES

A template allows you to preview how your design will look after cutting it out on a specific kind of fabric, such as a bag or a t-shirt. If you're making a bag with an iron-on design, it'll show you an image of your bag, and the design can now be placed on that template so that you can start planning the appearance of the bag in reality.

Templates will not cut out a real backpack for you, but they'll explain what the designs look like when they are cut out.

PROJECTS

If you're ready to start cutting, then go to "Projects." You'll choose your project, make edits, modify it to suit your taste, and then click the "Make It" option. Several projects are available for users with Cricut Access membership, and some projects are accessible by purchase only. Apart from both means, only a few projects are free.

IMAGES

Images enable you to spice up your designs by adding a personal touch. With this tool, you can insert images that are provided on the Design Space for you. Cricut even offers free pictures each week, though some of them come with the Cricut Access.

TEXT

The text tool enables you to include texts to your designs or only on the Canvas area. Clicking the "Text" tool opens a little window, indicating that you should add your text. You can add text and also customize the color and font.

SHAPES

This tool is used when you wish to add a shape to your Canvas area. The Design Space provides some shapes for its users: square, triangle, hexagon, pentagon, heart, star, and octagon.
There's likewise the "Score Line" tool located under the "Shapes" option. You can utilize this tool for folding these shapes to form other diverse shapes, particularly when you're making cards.

UPLOAD

The "Upload" tool is the last tool you'll find in the "Left Panel." This tool enables you to carry out file and image uploads, excluding the ones provided by Cricut. With this, images and patterns can be uploaded.

ELEMENTARY FUNCTIONS

Functions and tools are almost the same things. You can know the functions of a tool, and you can know the function of a function. However, what I regard as functions in the design space is to make

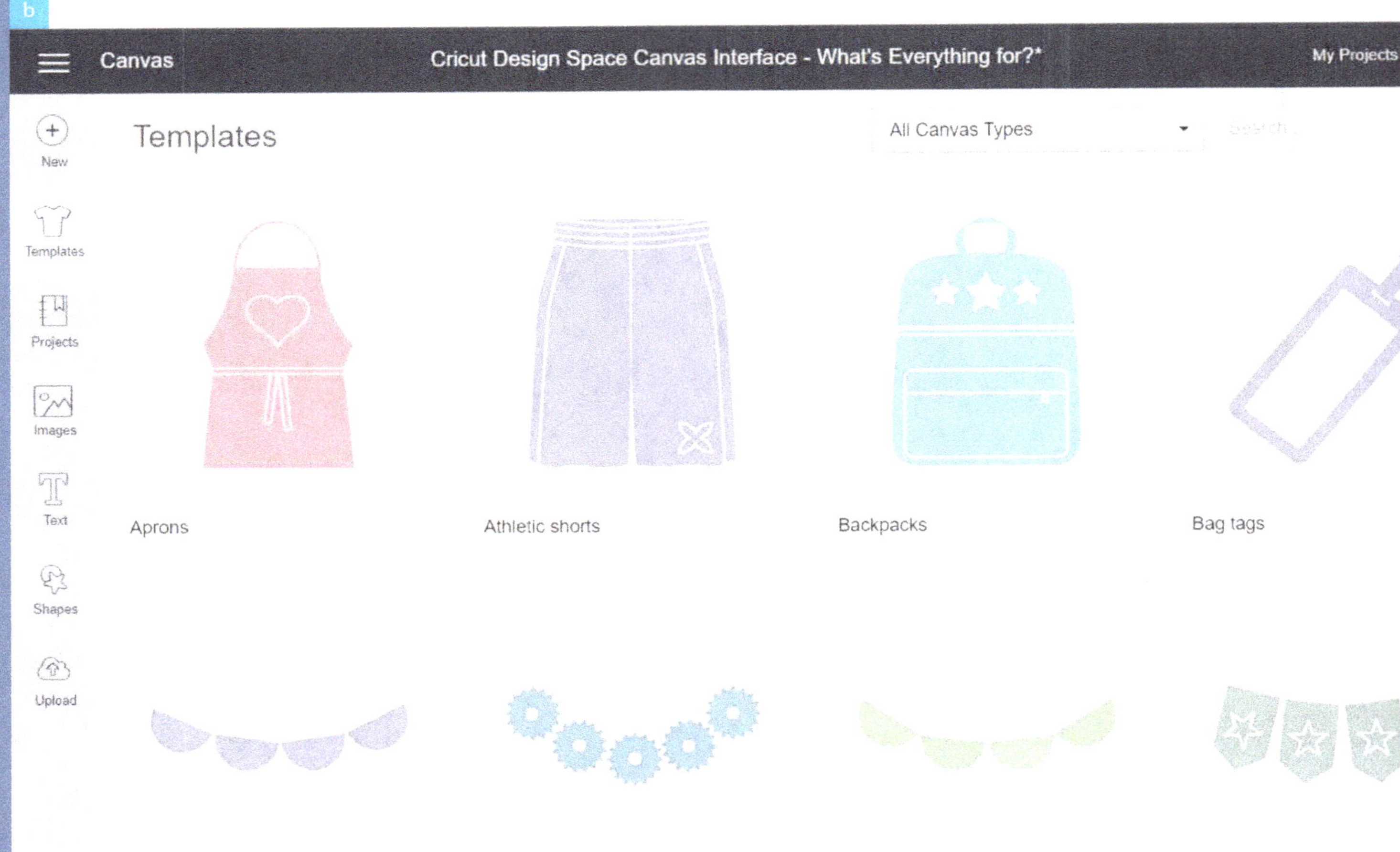

b
Canvas
Cricut Design Space Canvas Interface - What's Everything for?*
My Projects
New
Templates
Templates
Projects
Images
Text
Shapes
Upload
All Canvas Types
Aprons
Athletic shorts
Backpacks
Bag tags

edits, organize, or tweak the Canvas area. Let's proceed and check out some of the general functions of the Cricut Design Space.

TOP PANEL

The Top Panel is the only pane that is always full of activities. The Top Panel is for organizing and making general editing on layers of design and elements.

FIRST SUBPANEL –

This enables a user to name their projects, save them, and finally cut it. You can also find the options to save, name, and send your project for cutting on the Cricut machine in this subpanel.

· Toggle Menu: This option enables you to perform account and subscrption management. This menu likewise allows you to update your Design Space, calibrate your Cricut machine, and perform some other operations.

· Project Name: Apparently, you can use this function to name your project. The project's default name will be "Untitled," it'll always be like that until you rename it to something unique you can identify the project with.

· My Projects: This serves as a library for all your saved projects on the Design Space. So, this makes it possible to access old projects easily.

· Save: This option gets your project saved into the Design Space library. You should always save your work, so you will not have issues when your browser crashes or stops responding.

· Cricut Maker / Cricut Explore: When using

the Design Space for the first time, a question will pop up to inquire if you're making use of a Cricut Explore machine from the Series or a Cricut Maker. Cricut Maker stands as the most advanced machine made by Cricut, and therefore, it provides several benefits on the Design Space more than other machines you'll find in the Explore Series.

·   Make It: Click "Make It" after you've uploaded your files so that it can start cutting. The software categorizes your projects based on their colors, and if you're making plans to cut two or more projects, you can use this tool to increment the projects you wish to cut.

<u>Second Subpanel</u>

The second subpanel is a menu for editing. It enables you to arrange, organize, and edit fonts and images on the canvas area.

Undo & Redo:

Clicking "Undo" will revert a recent activity or action, and it's mostly used when a mistake is made or when an undesired move has been made. "Redo" does the opposite of "Undo," it brings back a deleted or reverted activity or action, and it's mostly used when something needed has been mistakenly deleted.

Cut Under (Line Type)

You'll find this line type on every layer present in the Canvas area. After picking the "Make It" option, your Cricut machine starts cutting the

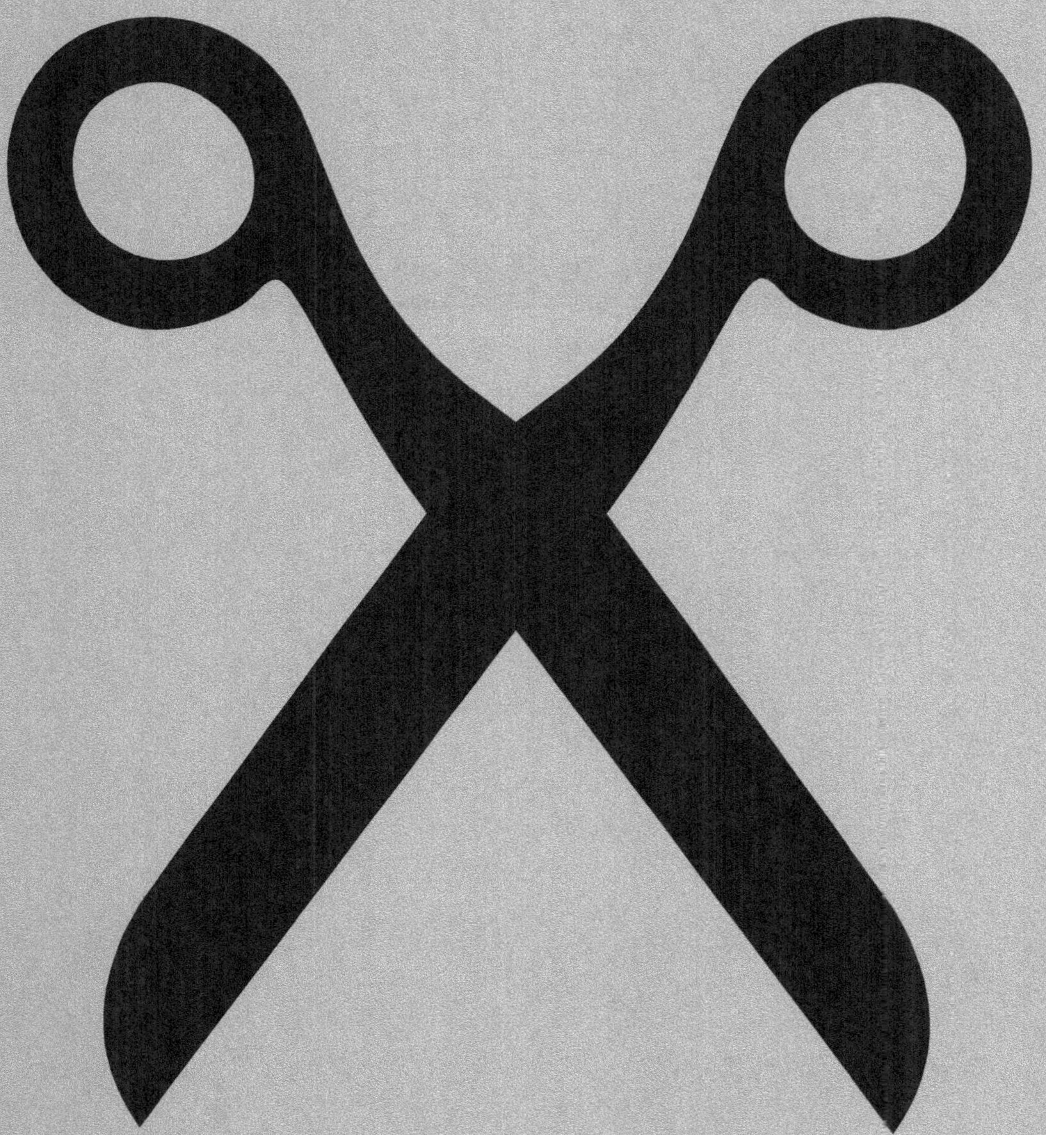

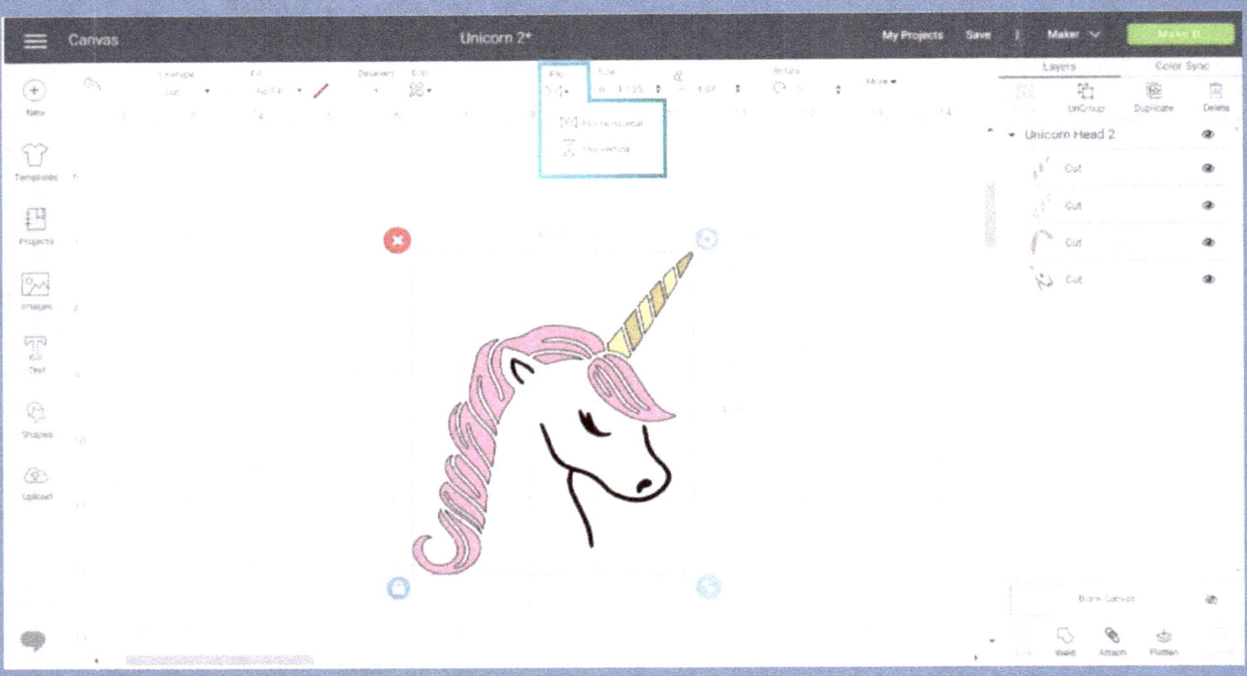

designs that are on your Canvas area. This function enables you to alter the fill and colors of your layers.

DRAW (LINE TYPE):

Cricut likewise enables you to draw and write on the designs you create. When you choose this Line type, you're given several choices of various Cricut pens. You can utilize these pens to make drawings in the Canvas area.

In this Line type, whenever you click "Make It," instead of cutting, your machine starts drawing or writing.

· Score (Line Type): This function does almost the same thing as the "Scoring Line" tool in the Left Panel; it's just more advanced. Selecting this function for any of your layers will make it look like the layer has been scored. After that, click on "Make it" will get the materials scored by your Cricut machine instead of having it cut

· A scoring wheel or scoring stylus will always be needed whenever you want to score. And only the latest machine, the Cricut Maker, can work with the scoring wheel.

· Engrave, Wave, Deboss, and Perf (Line type): These tools were recently released by Cricut. Therefore, only Cricut Maker users can make use of them. Additionally, it's required to have the newest version of the Design Space app before these new tools can be accessed. These tools enable you to make significant effects on many materials.

· Fill Cricut majorly designed this function

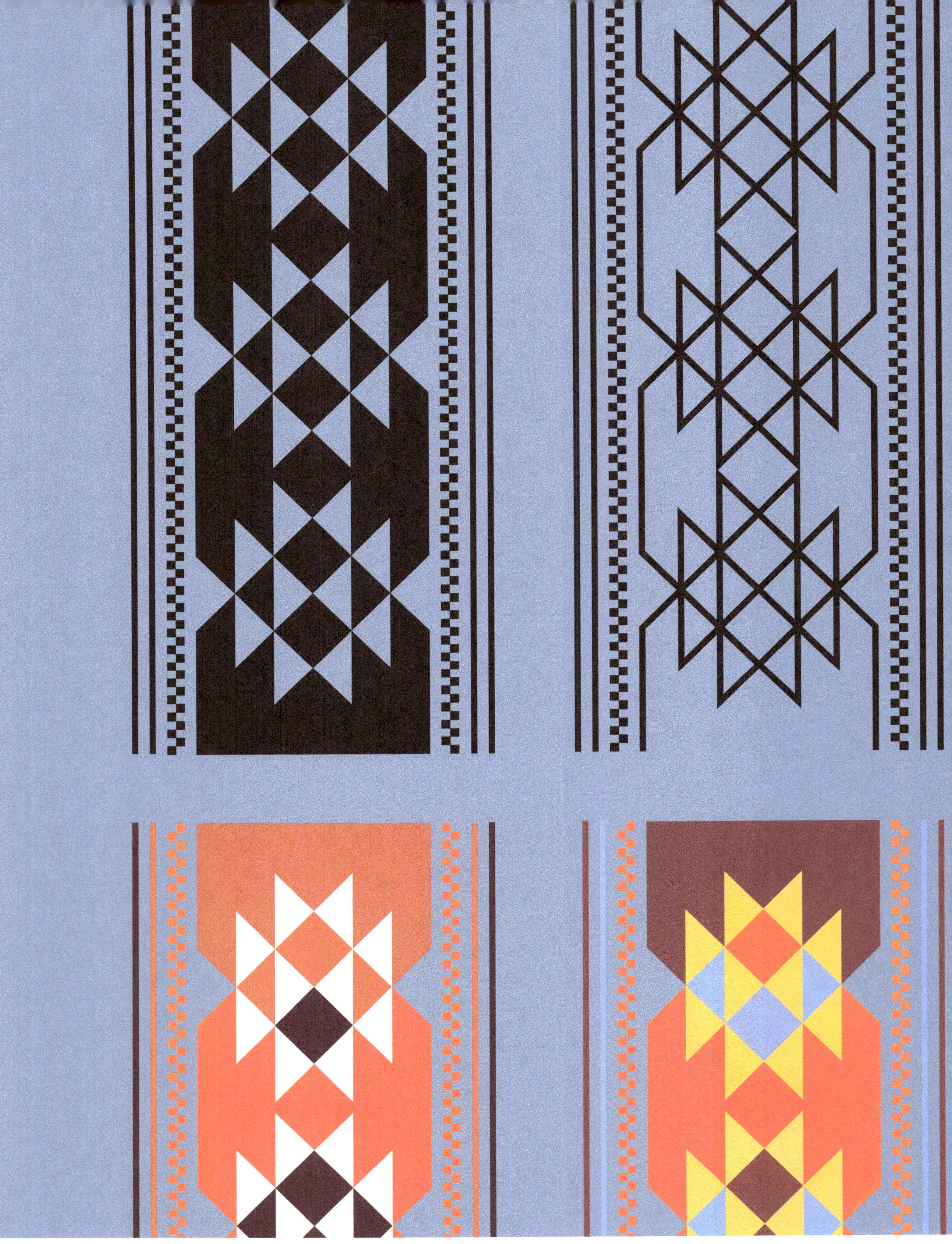

to print and make patterns. However, you can only use this function "Cut" has been selected as a Line type.

PRINT

Every Cricut user loves this function. Even though you cannot do without it if you want your design to be cuttable, you'll also find this function a little bit interesting.
It enables you first to have your design printed out and then cut them out. If you want to print out your design, click on "Make It" when the "Fill" option is active. After that, send the files to your home printer before you start sending them to the Cricut machine for cutting.

EDIT

This function consists of three options on the menu list. You'll find a "Cut" option, which enables you to copy. Clear elements from the Canvas, you'll find the "Copy" option, which allows you to copy the same component without getting it cleared, and lastly, you'll find the "Paste" option, which helps you insert the element you've copied or cut.
·   Select All: Clicking this will highlight everything you've on your Canvas area.
·   Align: There're several diverse options under this function, and it's essential for you to master all these options. Let's take a look at them:
·   Align Left: This function makes sure that every element is left-aligned. However, the movement will solely depend on the item at the end of the left side.

- Center Horizontally: This will horizontally align every design element.
- Align Right: This function makes sure that every element is right-aligned. However, the movement will solely depend on the item at the end of the right side.
- Align Top: This will automatically align all the selected elements to the Canvas page's uppermost part.
- Center Vertically: This will vertically align every design element.
- Align Bottom: This functions as the exact opposite of the "Align Top" function. It aligns elements or layers to the bottom.
- Center: Clicking this function will center-align all elements that are either vertically aligned or horizontally aligned.
- Distribute: This enables you to distribute the spacing between layers or elements equally. We have two types:
1. Distribute Horizontally
2. Distribute Vertically

FLIP

This function will allow you to see the reflection of your designs. You can see this function as a mirror-view of your designs. There're two options available for this function:
1. Flip Horizontal
2. Flip Vertical

ARRANGE

- The "Arrange" function enables you to arran-

Flip Horizontal

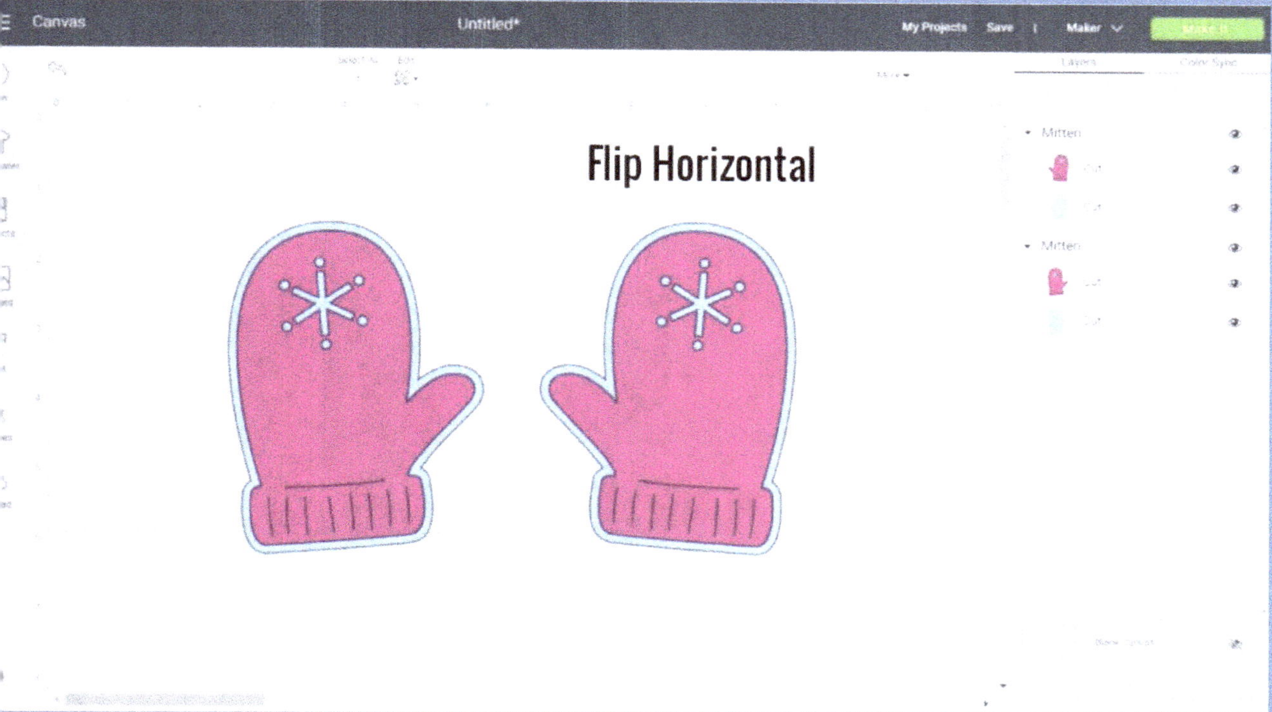

ge elements such as designs, texts, or images to the back or front of others. There're four types of arrangement, and they are as follows:

·   Send to Back: This moves the design or element you select to the farthest back of other elements or designs.

·   Move Backward: What makes this function and the "Send to Back" function different is that it moves an element or design back once. This allows you to control how further back you want an element or design.

·   Move Forward: This does the exact opposite of "Move Backward," you can control how further you want an element or design.

·   Send to Front: This moves the design or element you select to the furthest front of other elements or designs.

SIZE

This function enables you to alter an element's size or the whole design's size. Whatever you create within the Canvas Area has a specified scale, and you can use this to either decrease or increase the size. This is more useful when following a particular format for all the elements or the entire design.

ROTATE

With this Design Space function, you can rotate elements or layers to your desired angle.
Position
Since the Canvas area has gridlines, just like

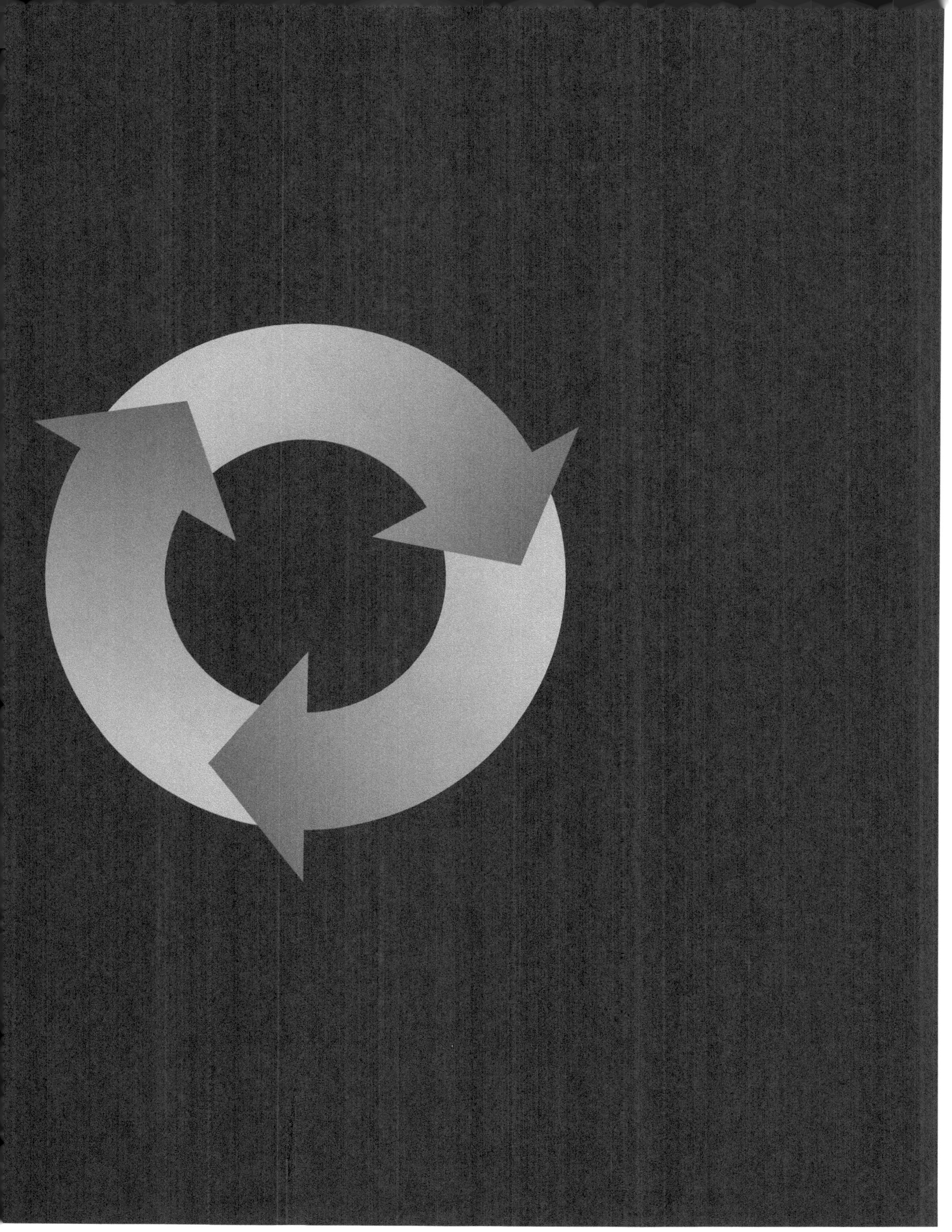

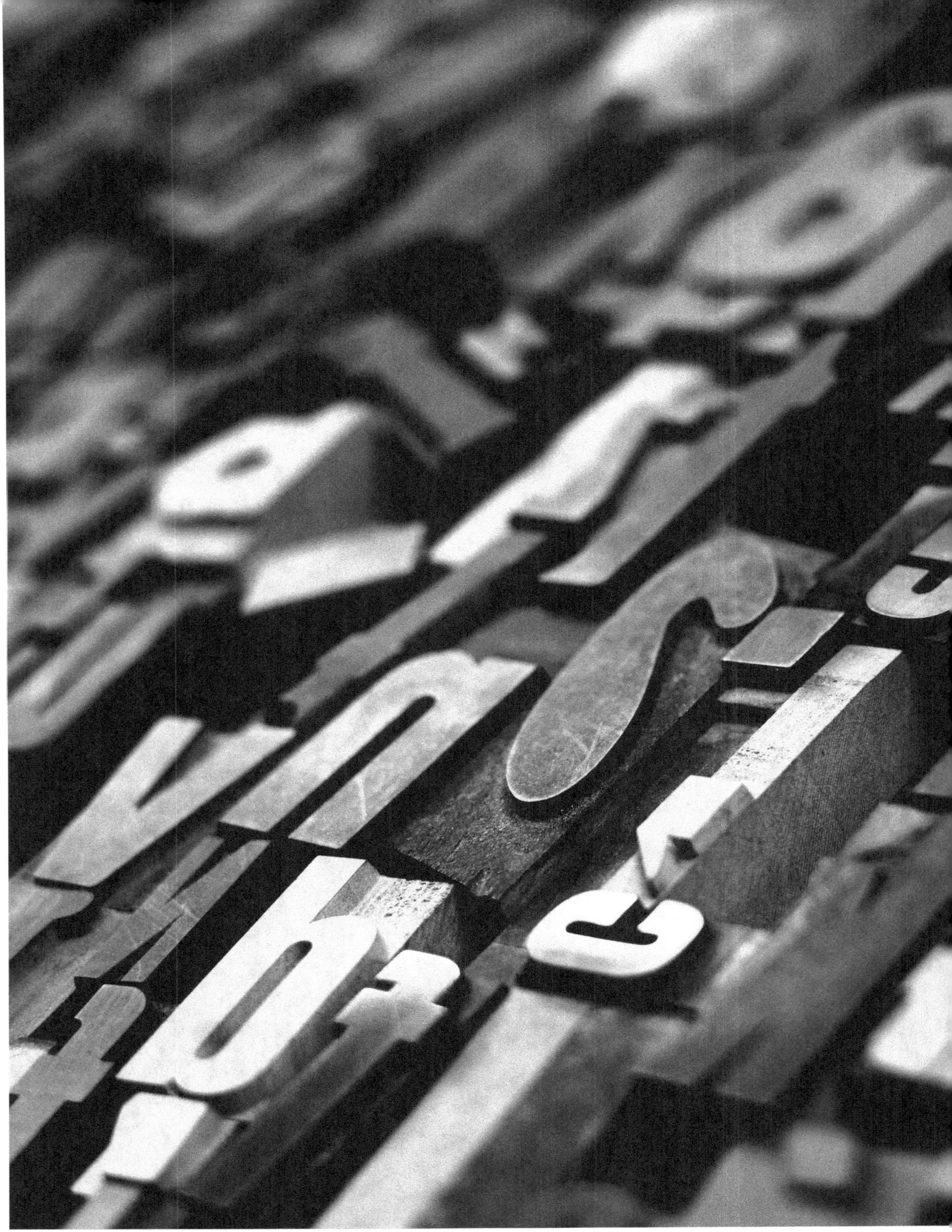

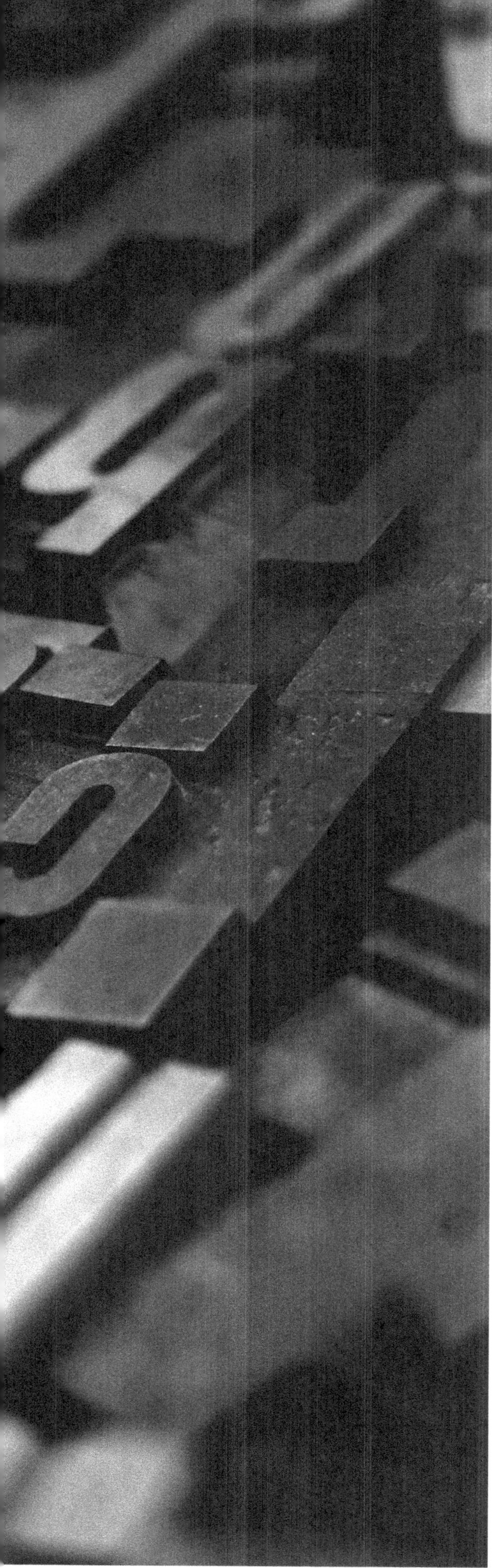

coordinates, you can use this function to find and pick a specific position for the element on the X and Y-axis.

FONT

There're various types of fonts on Cricut for all users with Cricut Access membership. You can use your default font or purchase different fonts from Cricut if you don't have a Cricut Access subscription.

FONT SIZE

This enables you to either decrease or increases your font size.

LINE SPACE

This is particularly suitable for use whenever you wish to make sure that all texts on your designs are orderly or manually spaced.

LETTER SPACE

This function enables you to decide how much space you want between letters.

STYLE

This consists of "Regular," which is already applied by default, "Bold," which makes the font thick, "Italic," which tilts the font sideways, and then "Bold Italic," which combines both the

Bold and Italic function.

CURVE

You can also design your texts by using the curve setting. You can curve your text upwards or inwards and also curve your texts into a circle.

ADVANCED

You'll find this function on the top editing panel, and it's the last function on the panel.

·   Ungroup to Letters: This enables you to detach all letters into single layers apiece.
·   Ungroup to Lines: Ths enables you to break paragraphs on different lines.
·   Ungroup to Layers: This option is available only on Cricut Access. It can also be purchased. It's quite tricky, though; you must be fully conscious of what you're doing
·

CANVAS AREA

This stands as the significant workspace of the Design Space. You can find all the designs and elements that you're working on on this platform.

CANVAS GRID AND DIMENSIONS

Gridlines are the lines that cover your Canvas Area on the Design Space and divide the area into small squares. The Canvas area resembles the cutting mat, which gives you the feeling of designing your actual cutting mat on the screen. You can use centimeters or inches, and you can also decide to turn the grid off in your settings.

ZOOM OUT OR IN

You can use this function to expand or reduce the focus of a design or an element on your canvas area. This function can be utilized if you desire to make your design bigger or smaller to work on it comfortably or if you just want to focus on a design or an element.

SELECTION

Whenever you select two or more layers, the color of the selection turns blue, and the four corners surrounding it enable you to adjust the layer. You'll see an "X" in red color; click on it when you want to delete those layers.

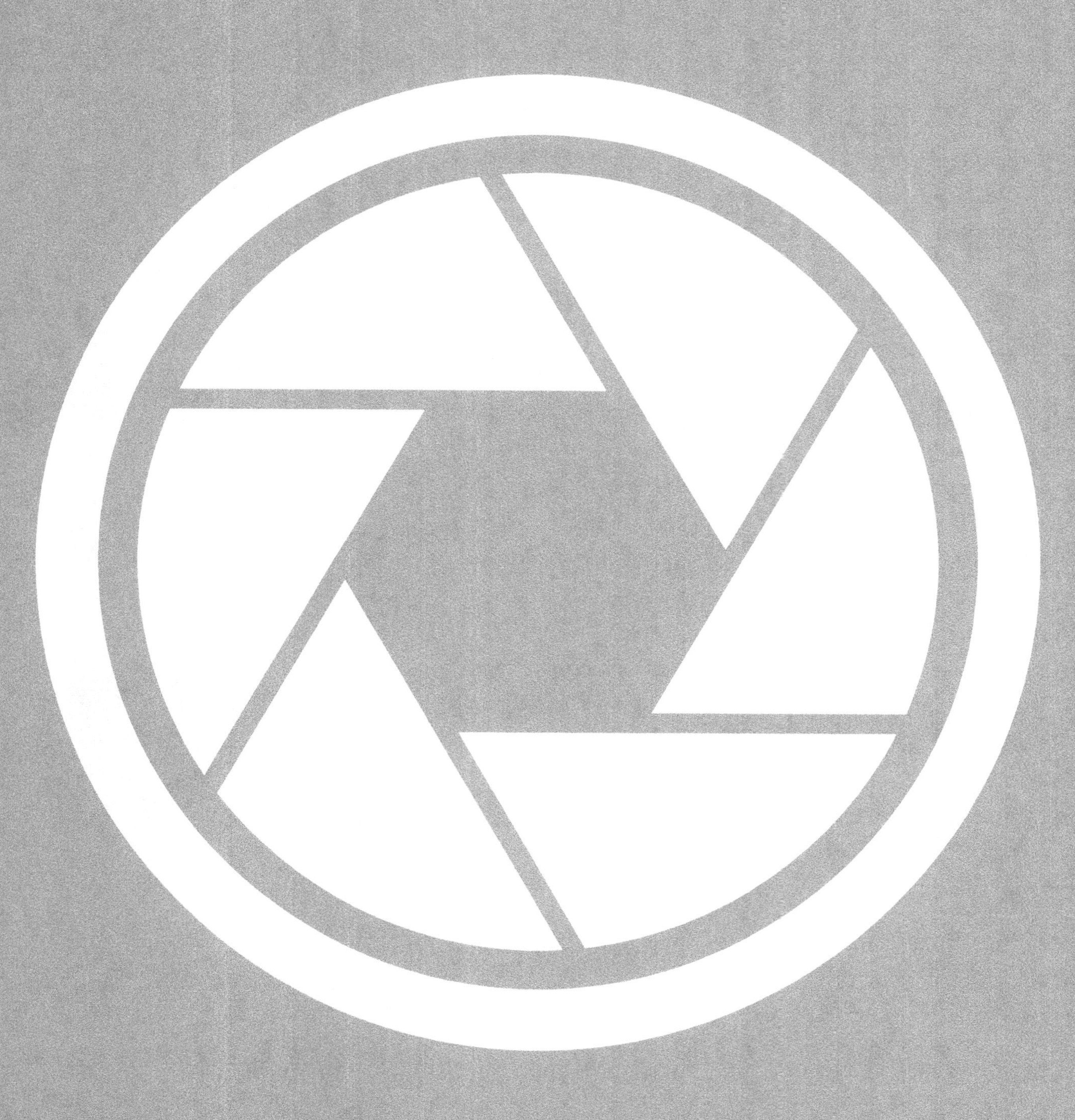

Chapter 4
Cricut Design Space 101

This guide will explain the program's rudiments alongside specific tips that will empower you to make unique designs with your Cricut machine.

STARTING POINT

Open up the Cricut Design Space. A screen like the one underneath. You can choose the "New Project" catch, or you can likewise peruse any of the Ready to Make extends in the "Highlighted Projects" zone. Arranged to Make tasks are projects that are as of now accomplished for you and are excessively generous.

You will see beside the "New Project." In case this is expected to make or alter one of them, you can likewise choose one of them.

When you select the "New Project," catch another reasonable canvas will open up.

On the left-hand side, you will see seven distinctive menu alternatives:

- New
- Formats
- Projects
- Images
- Content
- Shapes
- Upload

What all of these choices does in the going with

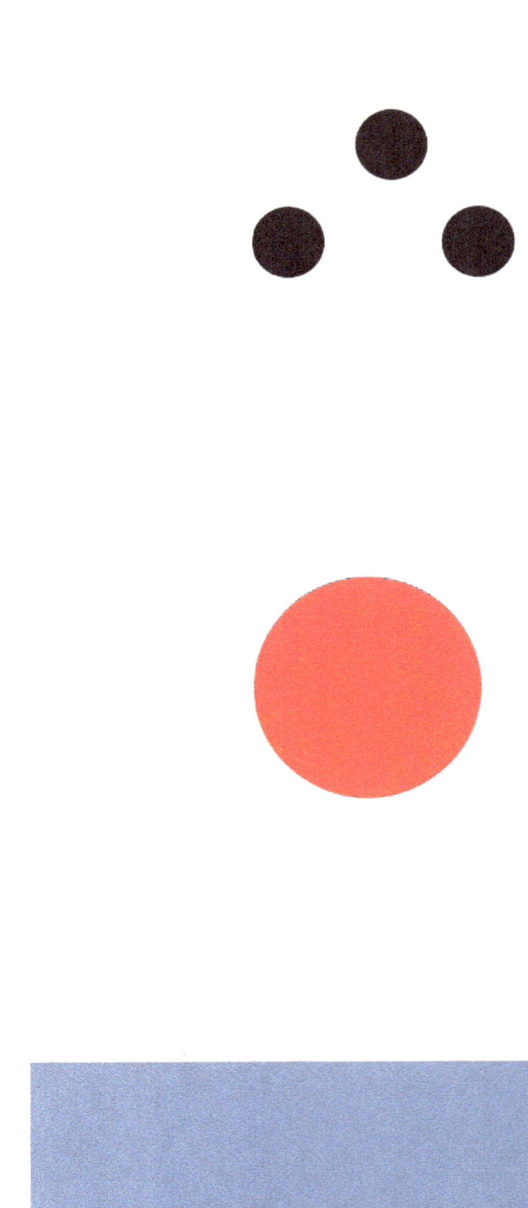

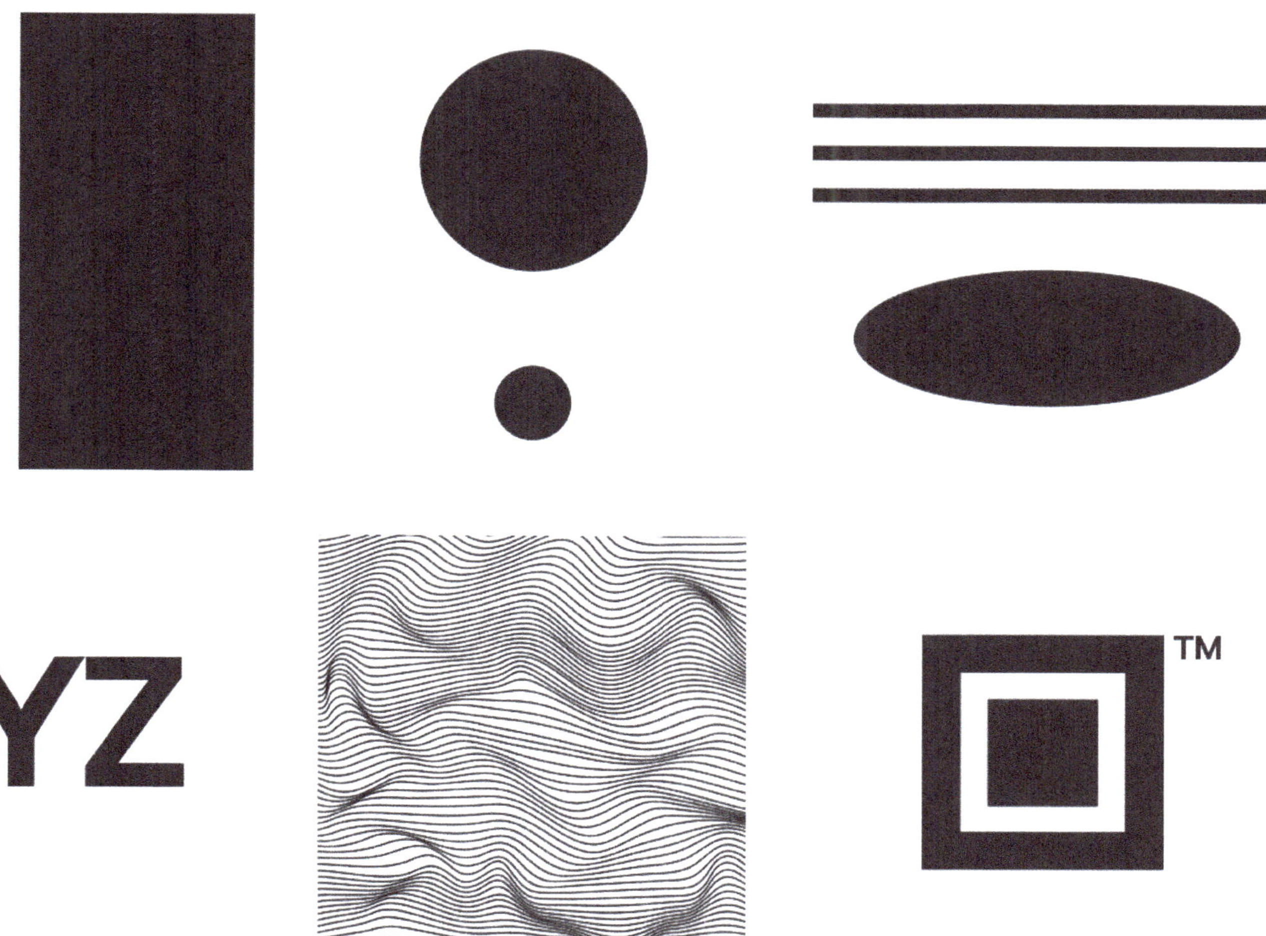

images is to explain the points.

"New" decision

Utilize this decision at whatever point to start another task and get a transparent canvas. After tapping on it, you will be incited if you have to spare your present task or supplant it with an open canvas.

FORMATS OR TEMPLATES TOOL

This is where you can set a particular kind of format to picture how your design will look on a specific thing. It very well may be useful for separating and estimating.

You can change the estimating in the drop-down menu to coordinate what you are going after on a portion of the formats. In the model beneath the cover, the size can be changed from Adult to Kid.

PROJECTS

Utilize this alternative to see all the accessible Ready Do Projects. These are projects that are as of now finished for you, and you can make them! A portion of the activities is adaptable once you open them.

You can scan explicitly for undertakings included with Cricut Access by utilizing the drop-down menu. For example, there are also different classifications, "Free for Cricut Maker" or "Free for Cricut Explore". These free projects are extraordinary to give it a shot on the off chance that you are merely learning to utilize your machine.

INSERTING IMAGES TOOL

After you click on the Images tool, you will see the Cricut library of images open. This is the place you can choose from with a vast number of images that can be embedded in your undertaking. To limit your choice on the upper right-hand side, there is an inquiry choice where you can scan for a particular picture. The images with the green "an" in the left corner are incorporated with your Cricut Access. Another slick choice is looking through explicit classes or cartridges. You can look into that particular one on the off chance that you had a more established Cricut cartridge you used to work with. You can likewise look through Categories, for example, "bloom."

TEXT TOOL

When you select this choice, a content box will show up, and you can type your ideal content. The content you composed will, at that point, show up on your canvas.

To edit your content, you will utilize the toolbar's choices over the top when your content is chosen. In the first drop-down box in the template, you can change your Font. You can choose from All Fonts, System Fonts (which means ones from your PC), or Cricut fonts to peruse. You can likewise utilize the quest bar to search for a particular font.

An extraordinary element is to utilize the Filter alternative on the extreme right half of the content menu. This enables you to channel your pursuit. You can choose only one channel, or you can choo-

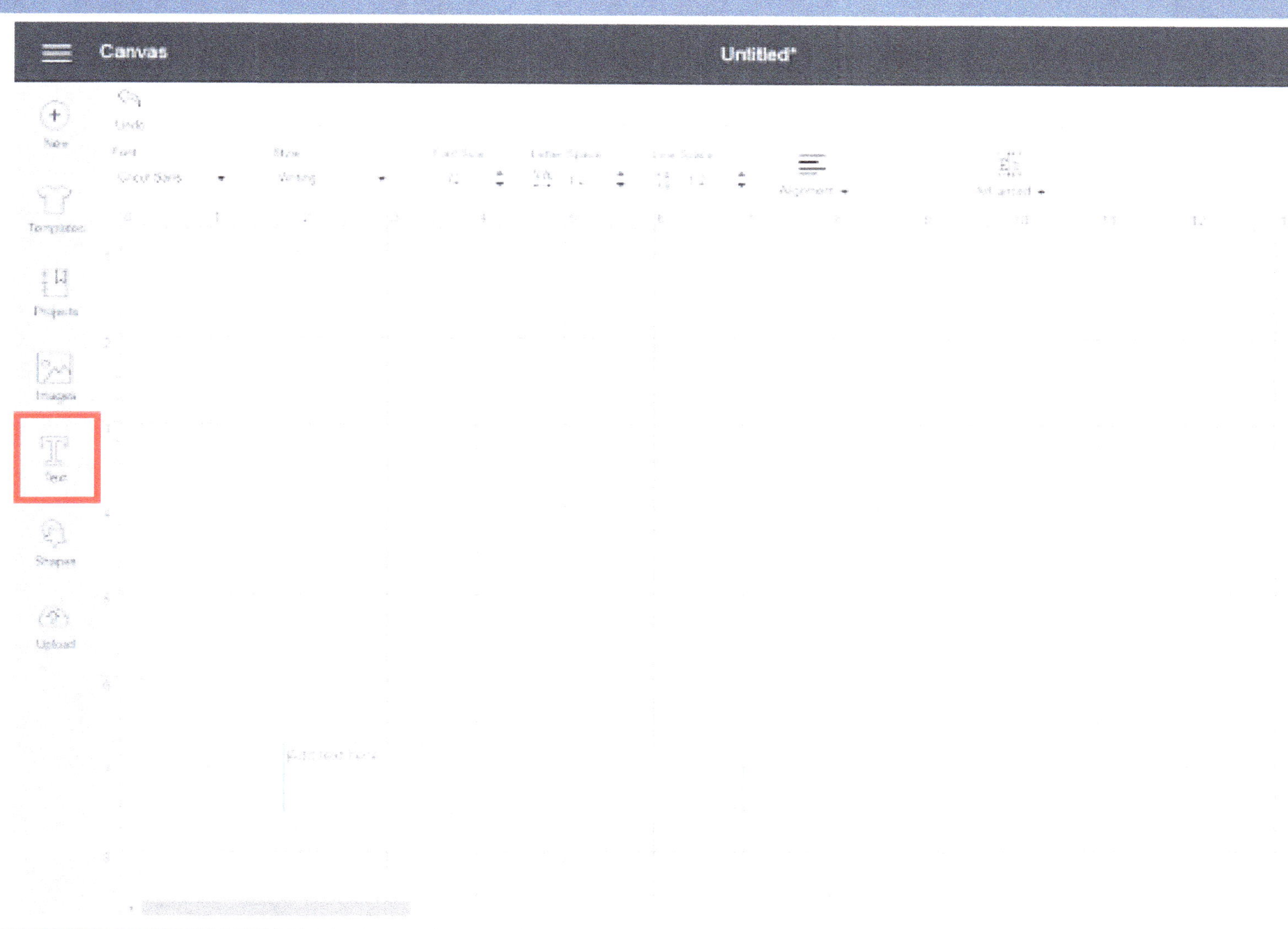

se numerous criteria, for example, "My Fonts" and "Composing." This will then show results that meet both of those criteria. Composing is an incredible one to channel on the off chance you are searching for fonts to utilize your Cricut pens. In the model underneath, choose "My Fonts" and "Stating" as my channels, so the main ones that appear meet those two criteria. Click the choices again to deselect them on your channels.

Multi-layer fonts are the ones that have a shadow. When you type your content, the default is that the shadow layer is covered up. You can tap on the eye symbol to demonstrate the shadow once more. However, if you chose a multi-layer font underneath, the shadow layer is covered until you click on the eye symbol and have it demonstrated once more. You will likewise see some other content choices, for example, Font Style, Font Size, Letter and Line Space, and Alignment. These are choices you are most likely used to. However, you can click around for a couple of minutes and accuaint yourself with them. Letter Space is an incredible tool to utilize when you have cursive letters, and you need them to be nearer together so they contact. Just decline the letter dispersing by choosing the sliding bolt. You can see that you can diminish the letter space for the word beneath. The Font you have selected from beneath is a "Stating" style font, which means you can utilize pens for composing when you make your task. Fonts that don't have a composition style will outline the content (the content isn't filled in when you make an undertaking).

Another essential tool is the seclude letters catch. You can utilize this to alter each letter independently in your content. You can use this to have the option to turn your letters on the off such that you need to make the content bent. Or, on the other hand, if you need a specific letter to be bigger, at that point, the rest. You can likewise choose your content on the canvas and right-click on your mouse to choose "Ungroup," which also does. When you are finished altering the content, select it once more, right snap and snap bunch so the entirety of your content can be moved and altered together once more.

In the picture over, your letter is secluded, so you can choose every one independently and turn or rotate them.

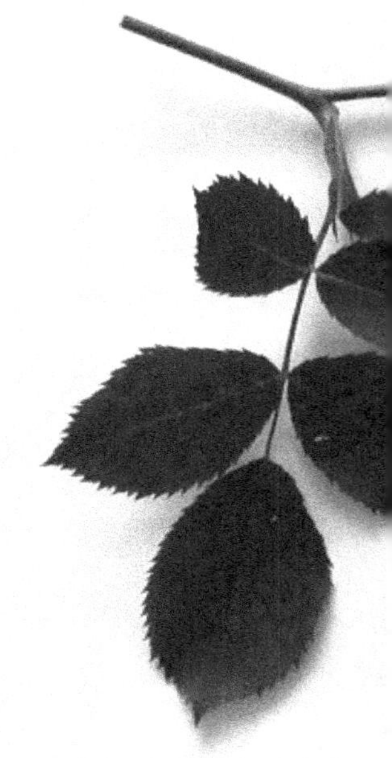

SHAPES TOOL

You can utilize this alternative to embed fundamental shapes into your design like a circle, square, heart, and so on.

UPLOAD TOOL

This is the place you can upload your unique images and Cricut designs. When you select and click on it, you will see this screen beneath.

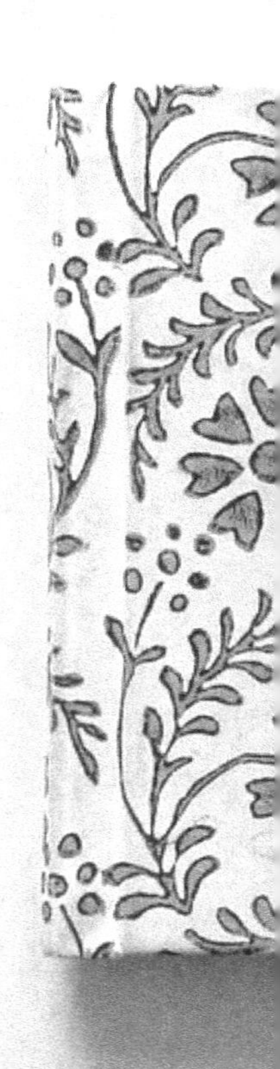

LAYERS MENU

If you have the Layers Menu open on your screen's right-hand side, you will see various choices on the base Slice, Weld, Attach, Flatten, and Contour. These will be significant when you are making your designs.

1.   Cut-Split two covering layers into parts.

2.   Weld-Join various layers into one shape

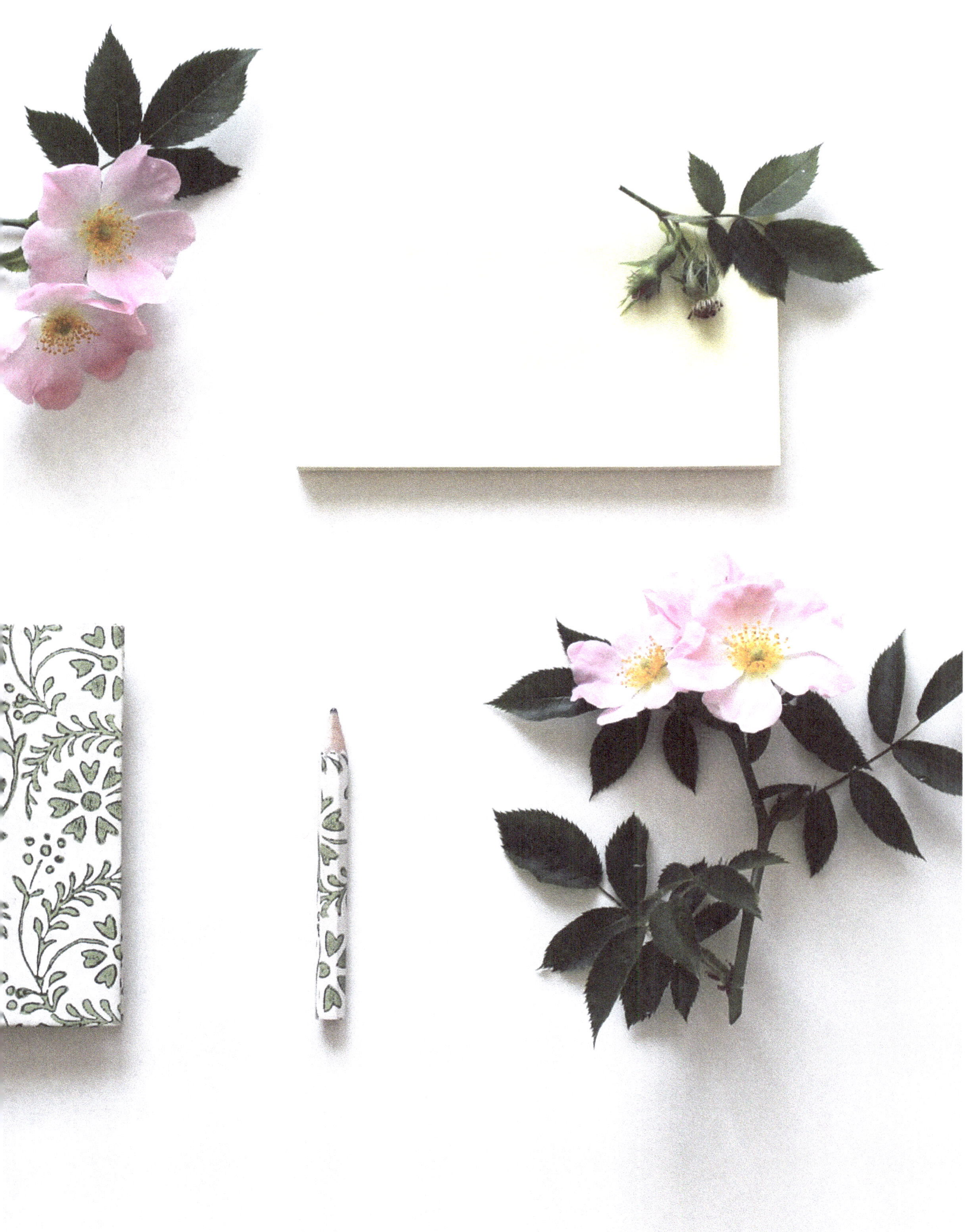

3.   Connect Hold images into position for cutting, or adds writing to picture layer

4.   Straighten Merge layers to a solitary printable picture

5.   Contour-Hide/Unhide lines on a layer

The Layers menu will demonstrate the majority of the various messages and images you have on your canvas. Each is its layer. When you click on one of the layers selected, a menu box will spring up entitled Layer Attributes. This is the place you can change the traits of the layer you have chosen.

There are four unique choices Cut, Write, Score, and Print. If you look to one side of your layer you have chosen in the image; you will see the circle symbol's scissors. That implies your circle is right now set to Cut. If you select an alternate choice, for example, Write, that little symbol will change to the Writing symbol, a hover with a bit of pen tip in it. If you select the Print choice, the circle will be printed rather than cut or composed.

SHADING SYNC TOOL

Another choice is the Color Sync tool. It has a concise depiction directly on the menu of what it does when you select it. You can relocate various layers to make them a similar shading. This helps when you are removing projects with different hues since it will guarantee you are cutting every one of the pieces that are the same shading simultaneously. This will spare you such a considerable amount of time to exchange the materials you are reducing and forward because you will cut no different shading simultaneously.

When you embed a shape or design, you can tap

on the little lock base in the base left corner to open the form. This enables you to estimate the shape uninhibitedly. If you need an exact size shape, you can likewise choose the shape and change the menu numbers above. There are likewise alternatives to turn your shape or position it to a particular area.

There are three activities on the Layers Menu that I much of the time use, Slice, Weld, and Attach.

APPEND/ATTACH TOOL

If you need the Cricut to remove something precisely how you have it on your canvas, you will need to utilize the Attach choice. Such a large number of individuals get disappointed when they hit the Go catch to cut, and their design is moved around by the program to slice it to ration material. Dodge that issue by choosing Attach

CUT/SLICE TOOL

When you have two layers, you can choose both and select the Slice catch, which will part your layers into the image underneath. (Ensure you have your ideal layers chosen, as shown by being featured in blue on the layers menu.)

WELD TOOL

Again, you could choose both shapes and utilize the Weld capacity to make them into one form. You can use both of these alternatives to change your shapes and designs.

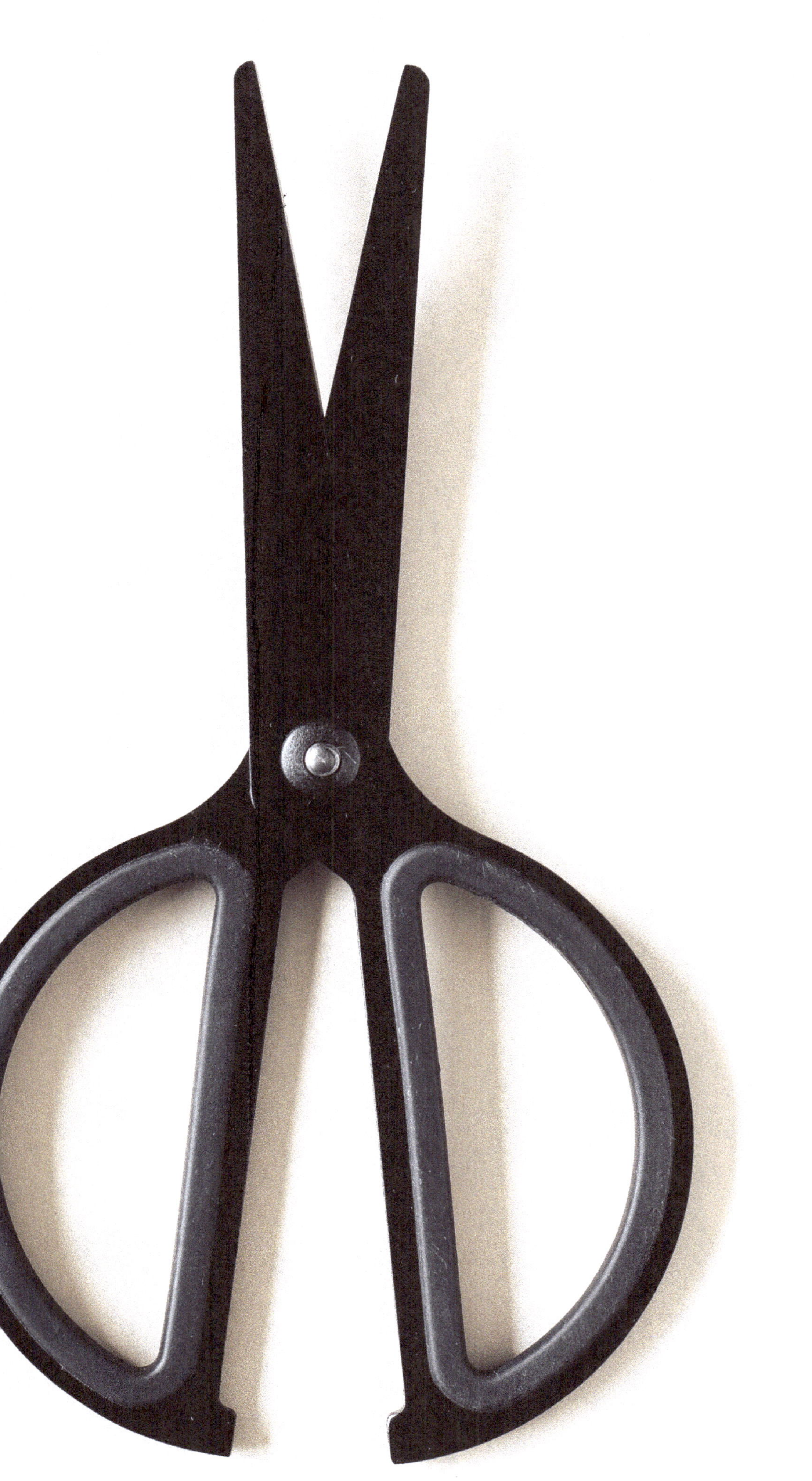

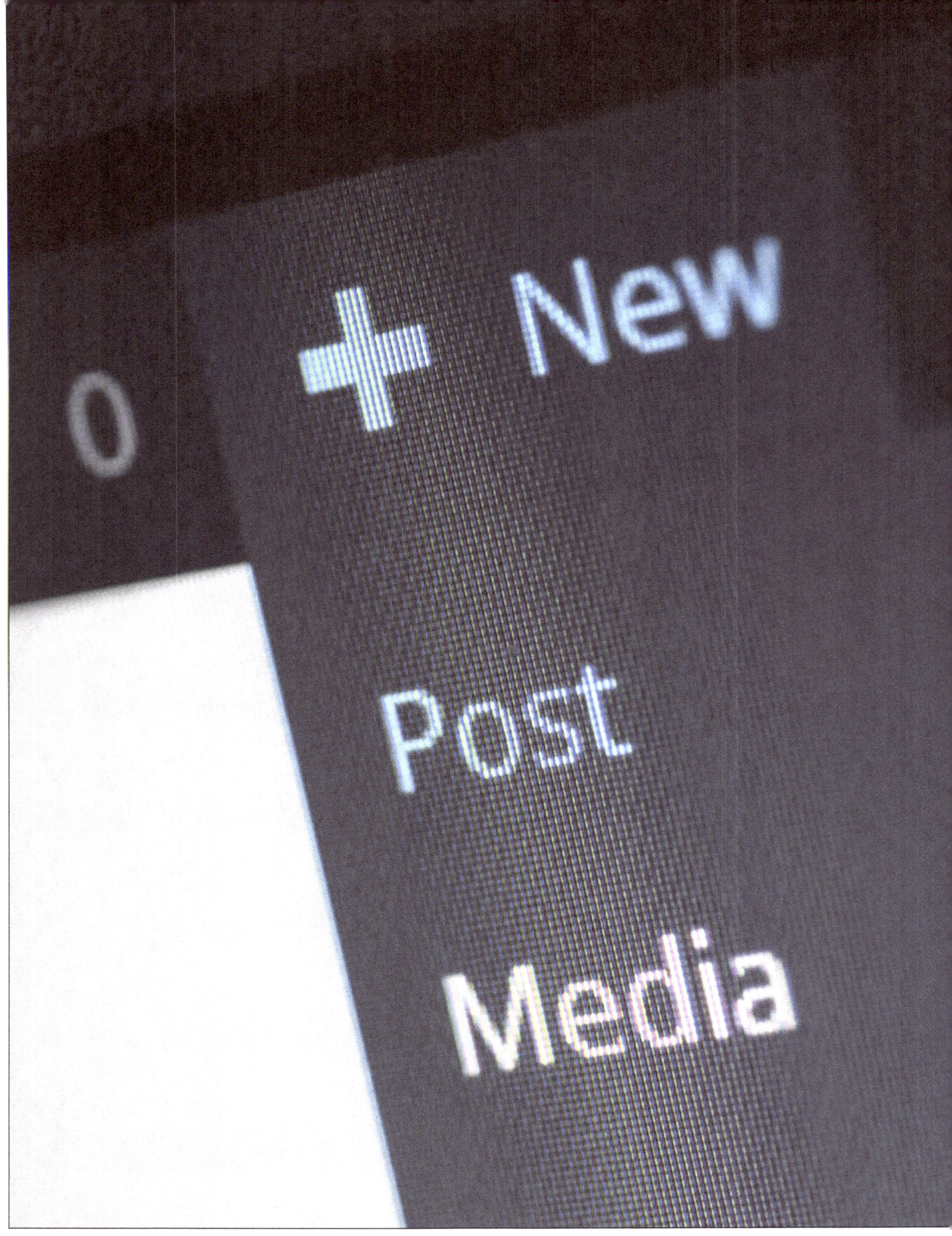
0
New
Post
Media

When you are prepared to do your project, you will tap on Make It in the upper right corner.

This will open the mat to see the screen where you can change a ton of choices. Above all else, when you click on your picture, three little spots will show up in the corner, and a bolt will likewise show up. The three small dabs give you the choices to move your picture to another mat or conceal it. (In this model, you have one knot at present. However, later on, in the model, you will utilize the move choice.) If you didn't need the chose picture to cut, you would choose the Hide alternative.

The round bolt on the picture's privilege enables you to turn your picture on how you might want it cut. You can likewise move your picture where you might want it on the mat.

Another effective alternative is Project Copies in the upper left corner. Here you can choose what number of duplicates you need to remove your picture. After you select figure 8 and hit apply, every one of the duplicates will populate on the screen, and you will currently have two mats.

If you needed to move one of the hearts to the main tangle, you will tap on the picture, utilize the three-speck choice to choose to move it, and after that select which mat and at that point, use the turning tool to make the picture fit on my first tangle. Design Space defaults to 12 X 12 material size; however, you can likewise change to your ideal size right on the review screen. Snap-on the drop-down menu and pick which size material you are utilizing. Below, assume you have chosen a 12X24 size, and now the entirety of your mind fits on one mat. The subsequent stage is to snap proceed and, after that, cut out my images.

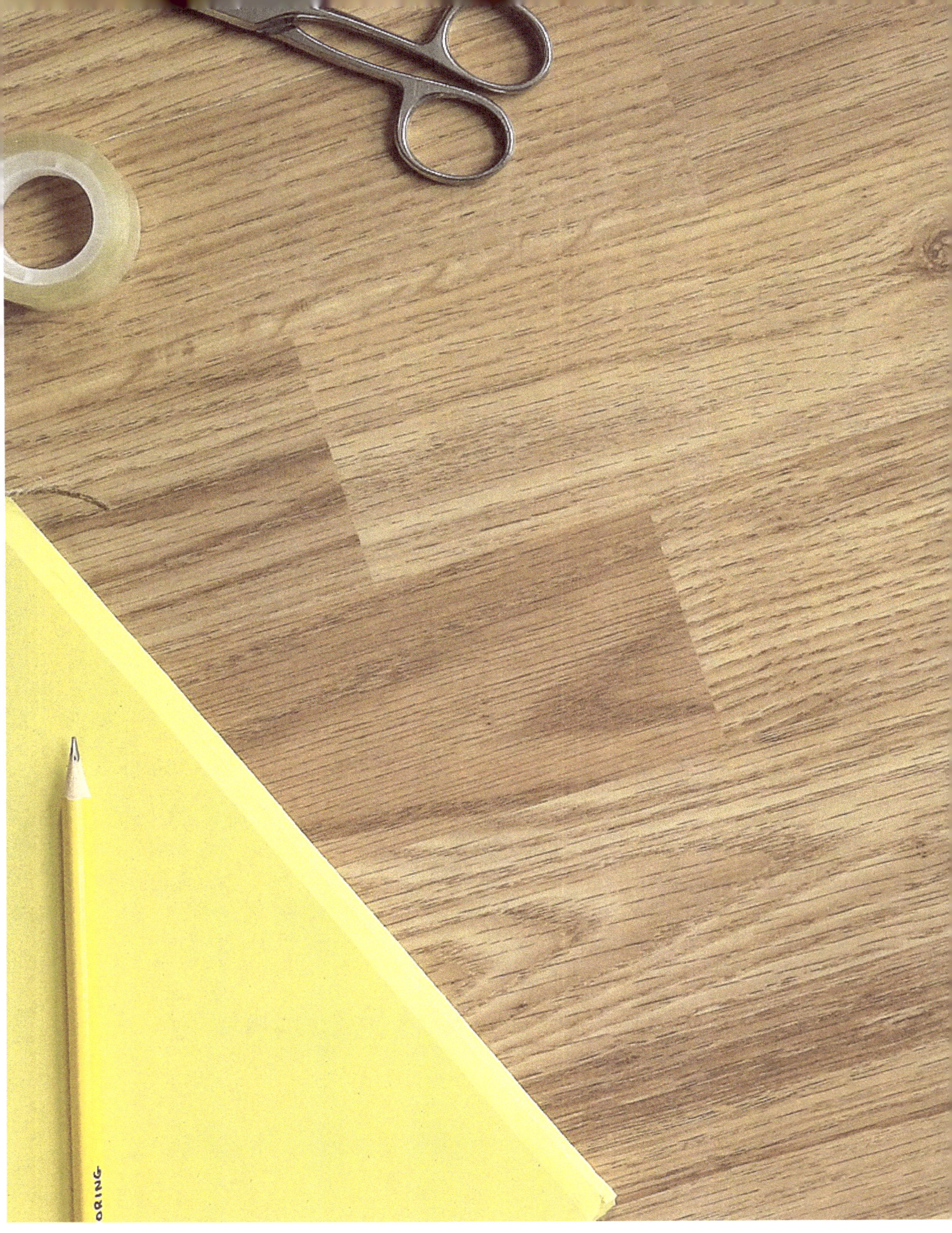

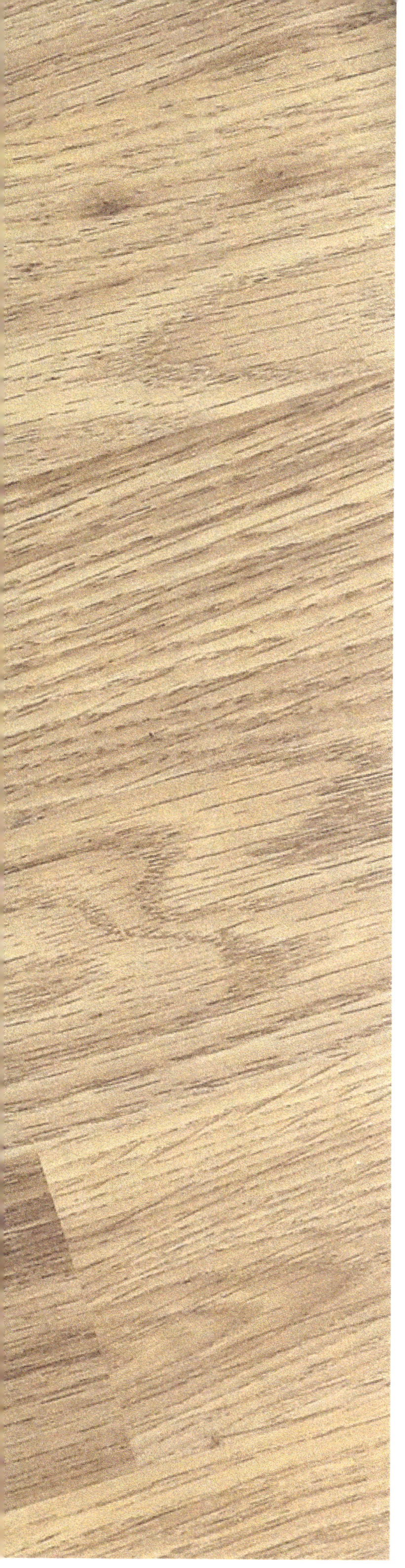

Chapter 5
Troubleshooting for Design Space

Is it true that you are having Cricut Design Space issues?

Is it stacking gradually, solidifying inside and out, slamming, or not opening by any stretch of the imagination? It's so baffling when this occurs because you simply need to continue ahead with your task, isn't that so? I know how it feels, and I'm going to give you a couple of tips on what to do about these Design Space issues.

Generally, Design Space is excellent programming. Indeed, there are a couple of more highlights we'd like to see included (it was extraordinary to get a bent book highlight as of late), however in general; it functions admirably for general extends. The most severe issue is smashing, slow stacking, solidifying, or not opening. We should investigate what you may have the option to do to fix these issues.

CONFIGURATION SPACE IS GLITCHY

-Check for programming refreshes, and download likewise
-Change programs
-Check web association

HOW WOULD I INTERFACE WITH BLUETOOTH?

- Enable Bluetooth on the gadget you might want

to interface your machine to

- Select your machine and enter secret word 0000
- Explore and Explore Air machines need a Bluetooth connector to interface with a Bluetooth empowered gadget

CONFIGURATION SPACE IS CHARGING ME FOR PICTURES I HAVE JUST BOUGHT/IM BOUGHT INTO CRICUT GET TO, AND IM BEING CHARGED FOR ACCESS PICTURES:

- Log out and log back into your record; plan space will once in a while sign you out without you understanding

SLOW INTERNET CONNECTION

The primary driver of issues with Design Space is a moderate web association. The program requires the excellent and reliable transfer and download speeds. A conflicting association with plunges and spikes may likewise mess up the product. You'll likely get an increasingly reliable association if your gadget is nearer to your modem.

Destinations like YouTube require great download velocities, and you can pull off a slower transfer speed. However, Cricut Design Space requires both download and transfer rates to be great, as you are continually sending and accepting data as you chip away at your plan.

Run A Speed Test

Run a web speed test with assistance like Ookla. Cricut specifies the accompanying prerequisites for Design Space to run well:

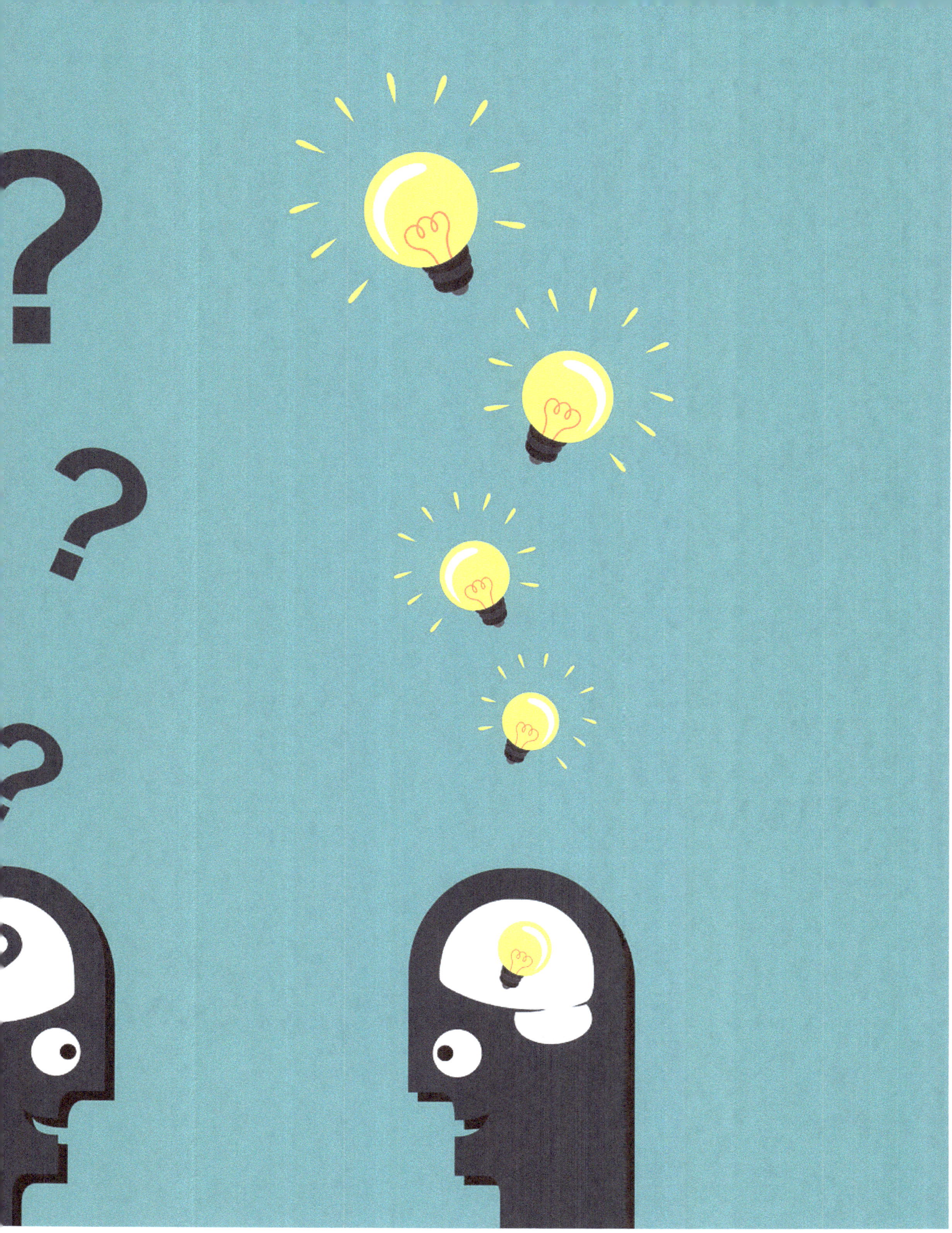

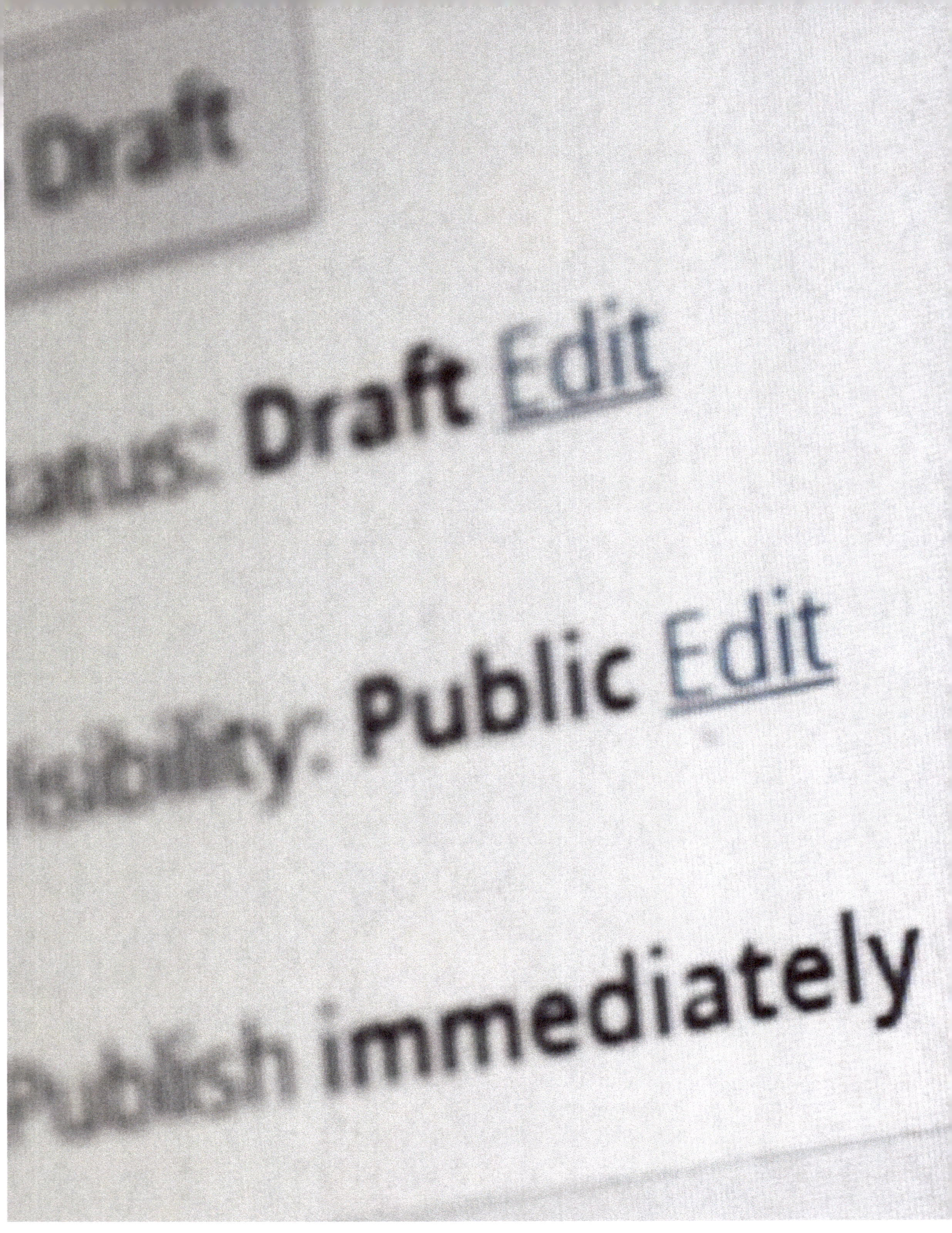

Draft

Status: **Draft** Edit

Visibility: **Public** Edit

Publish immediately

Broadband association

Minimum 2 - 3 Mbps Download

Least 1 - 2 Mbps Upload

If your outcomes are meager, and you feel that is causing or adding to your issues, call your network access supplier. It may be that you need another modem to give the necessary rates. That was my concern a year or two priors. Another modem ultimately tackled my issues - it's only an agony holding up a couple of days!

YOUR COMPUTER

If it's not your web speed, the issue might be the PC, tablet, or cell phone you are utilizing. There are prescribed least necessities for Design Space to run well. Here are the nuts and bolts:

Windows Computers

Your Windows PC should:

- be running on Windows 8 or later
- have Intel Core arrangement or AMD
  processor - mine has AMD and runs extraordinary
- have 4GB of Ram
- at any rate, 50MB of free plate space - the more, the better
- have a free USB port or Bluetooth association

Macintosh Computers

Your Mac PC will require the accompanying for Design Space to work:

-        a CPU of 1.83 GHz
-        the Mac OS X 10.12 or something later
-        have 4GB Ram
-        an accessible USB port or Bluetooth capacities.
-        have 50MB free space

FOUNDATION PROGRAMS

Another issue might be an excess of foundation projects running while you are attempting to utilize Design Space.

It is safe to say that you are at the same time watching Netflix, talking on Facebook, skyping your mother, downloading the last period of Fixer Upper, transferring your most recent Vlog to YouTube, all while attempting to structure a tee in Design Space? Other than meriting an award for having the option to achieve such a significant amount without a moment's delay, you'll have to close a couple of projects to get DS moving quickly.

However, all joking aside, it may be the issue, regardless of whether you're not doing all that. In some cases, merely shutting the things you're not utilizing will speed things up.

Different Things That Might Help

Here are a couple of different things you may jump at the chance to test out or complete:

-       clearing your store and history
-       check what your enemy of infection programming is doing and update if vital
-       update drivers (for Windows)
-       defragment your hard drive
-       run a malware check

These tests will help speed your PC up or may tackle the issue altogether.

YOUR BROWSER

Another conceivable reason for your Design Space issues could be your program.

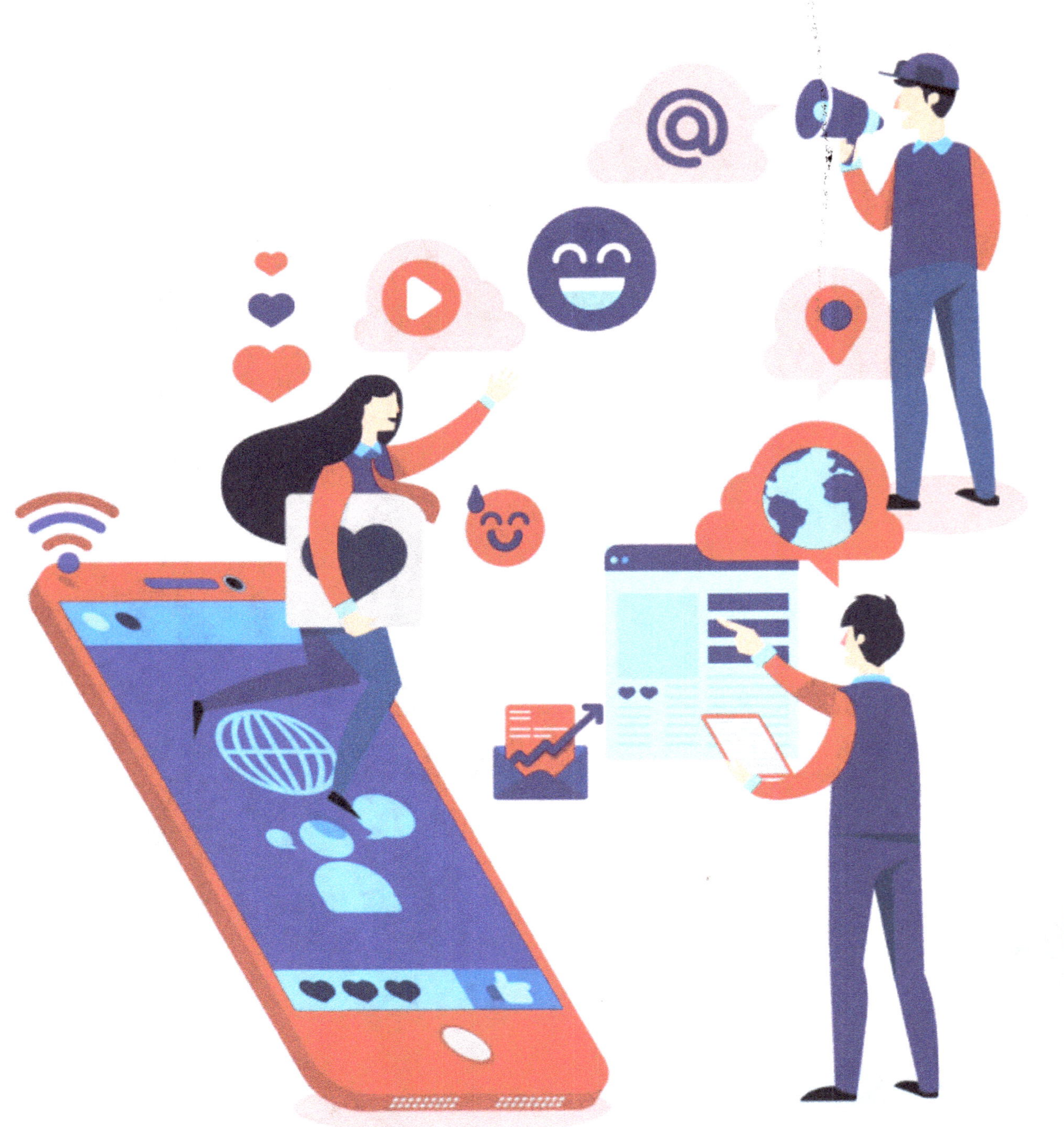

Cricut specifies you should utilize the most recent variant of a specific program. Regardless of whether you use Chrome, Mozilla, Firefox, or Edge, guarantee it is modern. If one program isn't working, check if it works in another. Now and then, for no good reason, this can take care of the issue.

WHEN TO CALL CRICUT

When all else fizzles, you may need to call Cricut client care to examine your specific issue.
I know there will be many issues that stay unaddressed here, so please leave a remark with what your battle is, and another person may have the option to support you!

Chapter 6
Cricut Alternative Software

It is no longer news that digital die-cutting units are incredibly restrictive for craft enthusiasts and people who love the Cricut die-cutting system.

They mostly allow users to cut a small number of fonts, and they are not cheap at all.

Thankfully, a few programs out there have managed to open Cricut to enable them to cut designs, TrueType fonts created by users, and many more. Below is a list of the best third-party software to use with Cricut.

MAKE THE CUT

This is an excellent third-party Cricut Design software that comes with simple but highly effective design features, e.g., it packs quick lattice tools, and it can convert raster images into vectors for cutting. The program has been around for some time. Some of the most outstanding features of the tool include:

•   It comes with advanced editing tools, and it is relatively easy to use (even for a newbie) because the user interface is effortless to learn.

•   The software works with many file formats, and it also uses TrueType fonts.

•   The software comes with a pixel trace tool that allows users to take and convert raster graphics into vector paths for cutting.

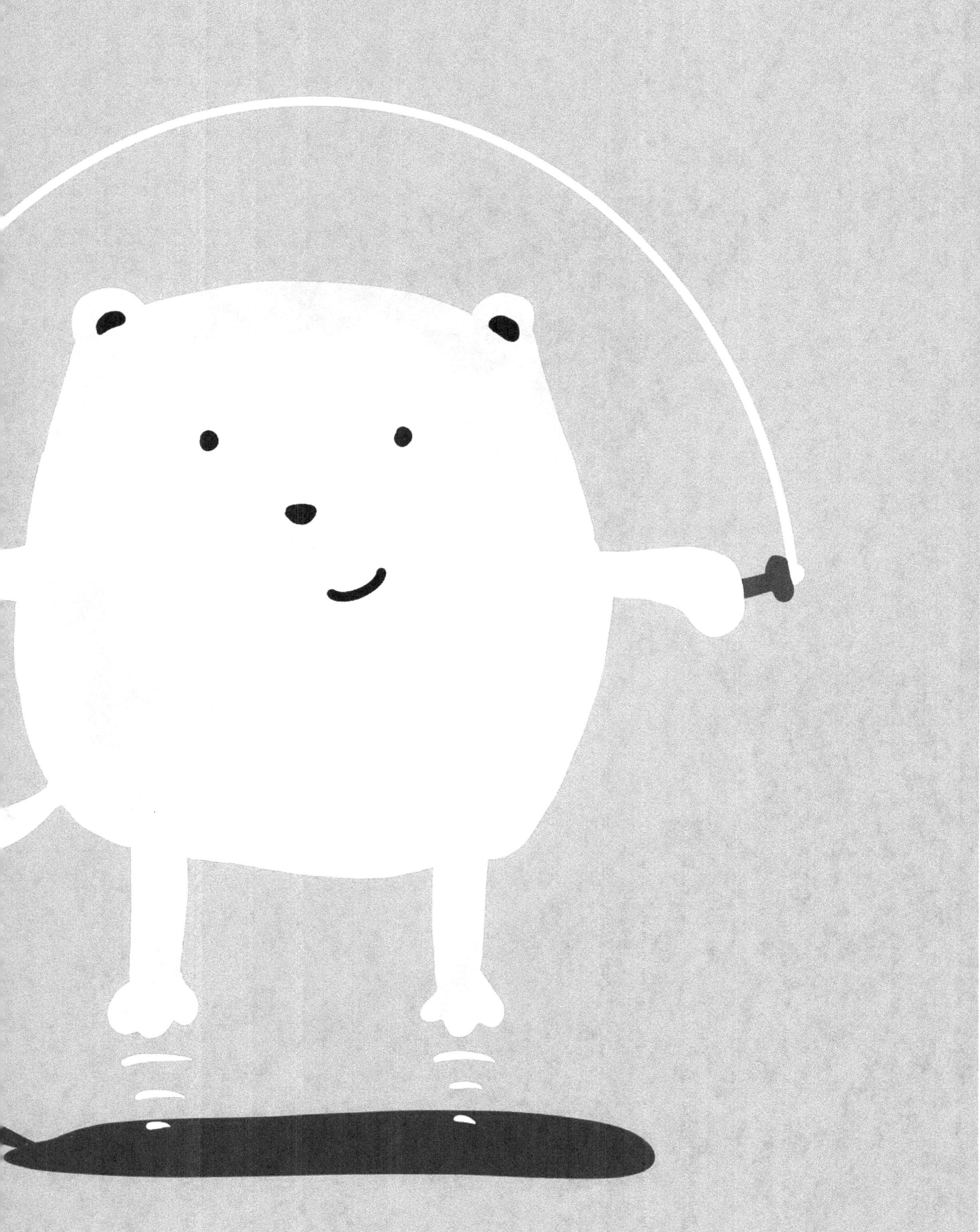

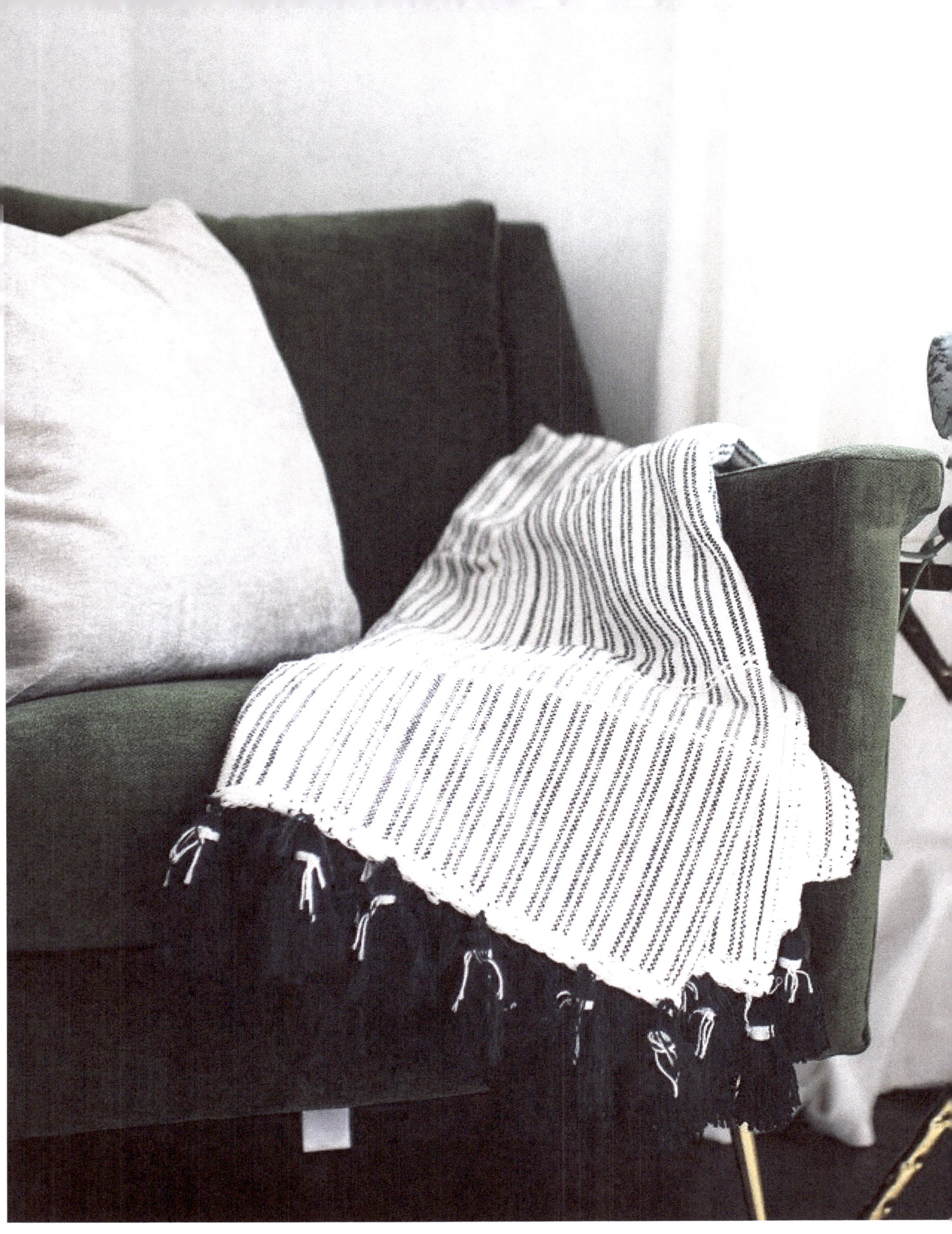

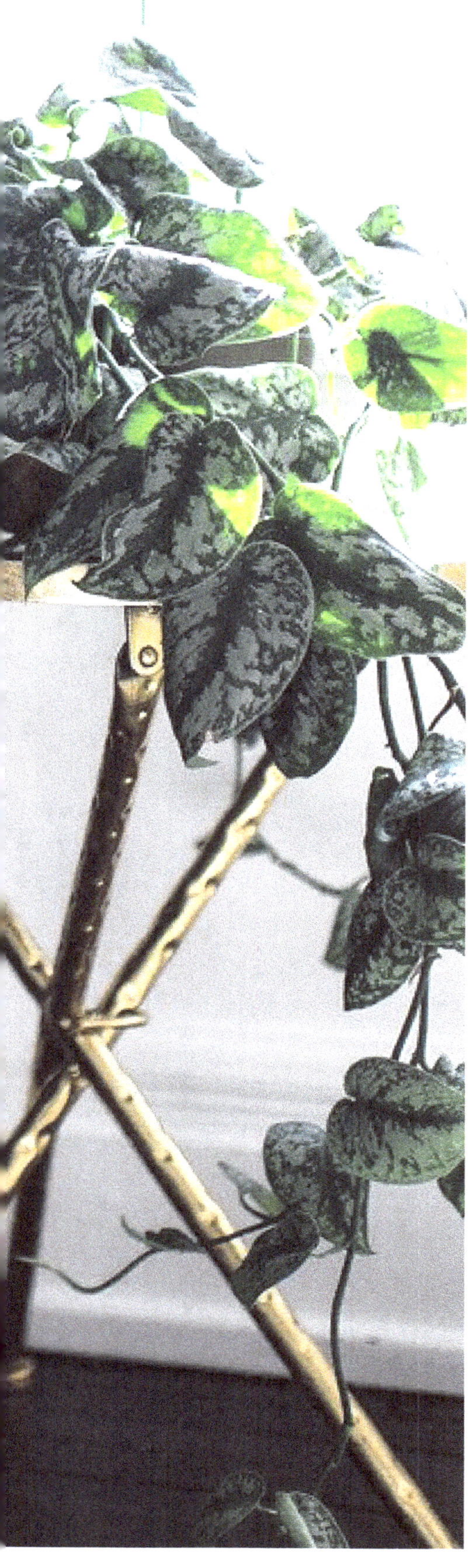

- For those that are interested, Make the Cut works with Gazelle, Craft ROBO, Wishblade, and Silhouette.
- Some other features include the fact that users can import the following: WPC, GSD, PS, AI9, EPS, OTF, TTF, SCUT, or PDF files and can also export shapes in SVG, Ai, EPS, PNG, and JPG formats.

Make the Cut is a user-friendly and flexible Cricut-related software that adds more utility to the digital die-cutting machine that is usually limited in usage and application.

SURE CUTS A LOT

The Sure Cuts A Lot of software gives users complete control of their designs without the cartridges' restrictions featured in Cricut DesignStudio.

Users must install a firmware update to their Cricut die-cutting machine; however, they can do this for free by downloading the trial version of DesignStudio. It is a straightforward task to perform.

Some of the features of the Sure Cuts A Lot software include:

- It allows users to use the OpenType and TrueType fonts.
- It is the one and only Cricut Design tool available that comes with freestyle drawing tools.
- It allows users to create unique designs with basic drawing and editing tools.
- The program works with Silhouette, Craft ROBO, and Wishblade die-cutting machines.

- It is specifically designed to open up all of Cricut's cutting features and abilities.
- It allows users to edit the individual nodes that make up the path.
- It comes with an auto trace feature that converts raster graphics into vector images.
- The programs have about 200 built-in shapes and other exciting features.
- It allows users to import different file formats, including PDF, SVG, AI, EPS, and WPC. The pro version allows users to import DXF and PLT.
- It allows users to select styles, including Blackout and Shadow, to quickly change shapes and letters with just a few clicks of the mouse.
- It allows users to use advanced features such as layers, grouping, and the weld tool to make the most out of their designs.

To download and get the complete set of Sure Cuts A Lot of features, you can check their website. The Sure Cuts A Lot program doesn't come with fonts; it only allows users to use the already on their computers.

Getting more fonts to your computer isn't a big deal because thousands of fonts are out there. Besides, you don't have to buy any special cartridges to get more fonts to your system.

CRICUT DESIGNSTUDIO

Cricut DesignStudio, a product of ProvoCraft, allows users to connect Cricut to a personal computer to

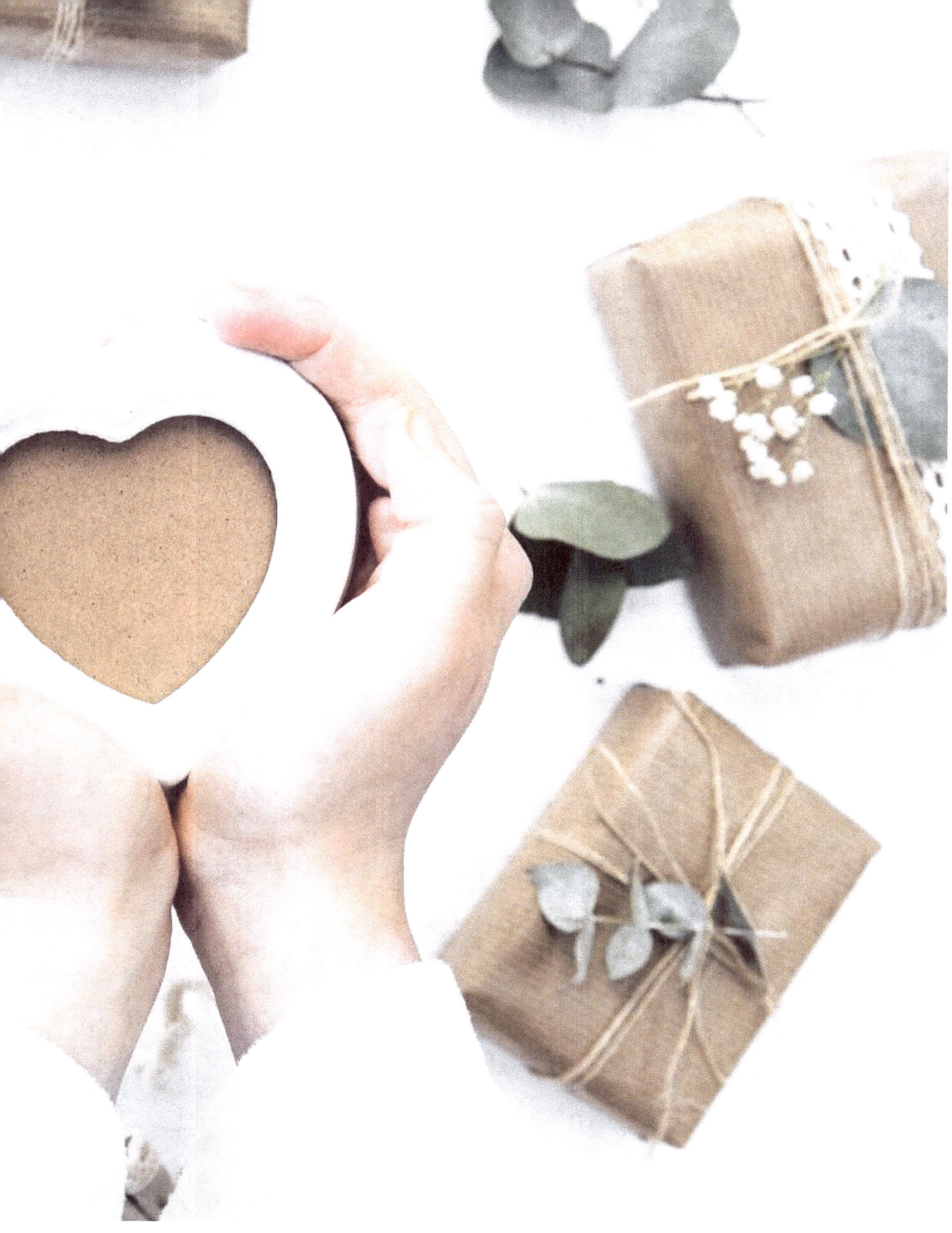

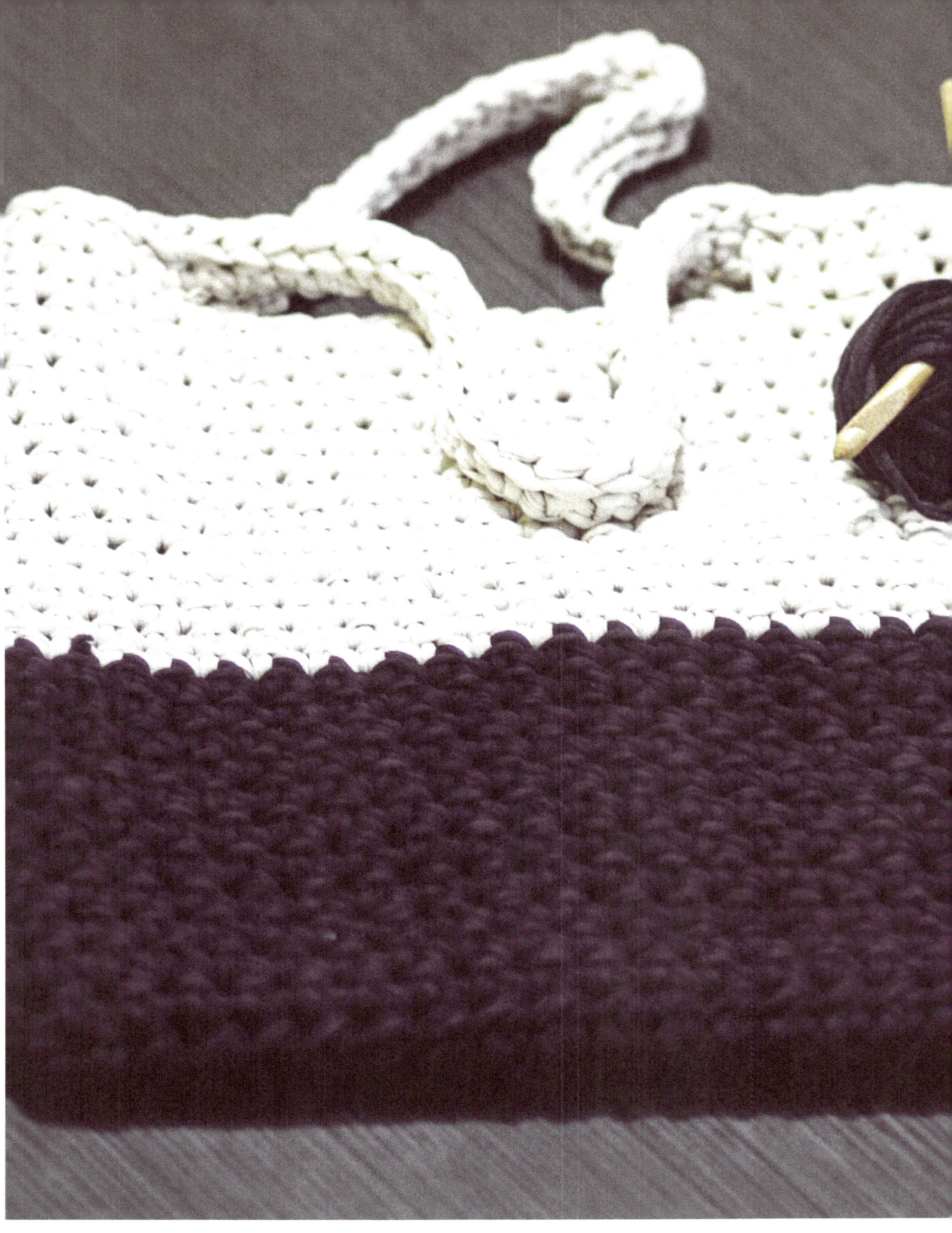

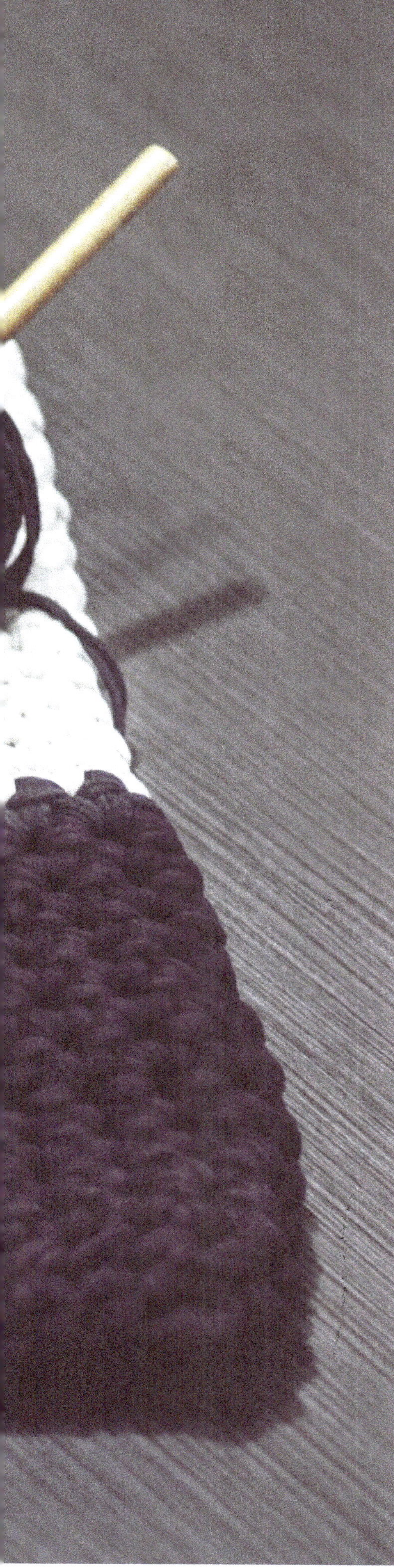

do much more with Cricut fonts and shapes.

For those that don't know, Provo Craft is the same company that manufactures Cricut die-cutting machines. With the aid of various tools, this Cricut software allows users to adjust fonts and shapes.

Some of the best features of the software include:

· Users will be able to weld, flip, and rotate easily.

· Users have the option of previewing and creating designs with different images from the Cricut library.

· Users will have to purchase a cartridge to cut.

· The software comes with a high level of customization to the Cricut library, and the extra features are beneficial.

· People who use this software are still limited to the same shapes and fonts from the cartridges they own but bearing in mind the tools packed in the program, which is not an issue.

The program remains a perfect option to use alongside your Cricut, and you'l be able to get the best out of its features. To know more about the software, go to their official website.

INKSCAPE

Inkscape is an open-source graphics editor for Windows and other operating systems. It is a professional program that costs absolutely nothing.

Users can use the program and Cricut to create and edit vector graphics such as illustrations, diagrams, line arts, logos, elaborate paintings, and much more.

Below are some of the features that come with the software:

· It can be used to render primitive text and vector shapes.

· It supports embedding and optional tracing of raster graphics.

· The objects can be filled with solid colors, patterns, radial, linear color gradients, and others; their borders can be stroked with adjustable transparency.

· The program can be used to create vector graphics from multiple raster sources and pictures.

· Shapes created can be manipulated easily with different transformations: moving, rotating, scaling, and skewing.

There are many more features present in this powerful software, and the easiest way to get acquainted with them all is to visit Inkscape's official website.

To maximize the use of your Cricut machine, you should consider using these excellent software applications that are compatible with Windows systems.

For the best experience possible, you should pair them up with some 2D digital pixel art tools or with some photo editors.

Depending on what you choose to do, you will quickly take control of your creativity and use Cricut Design Space the way you've always dreamt of.

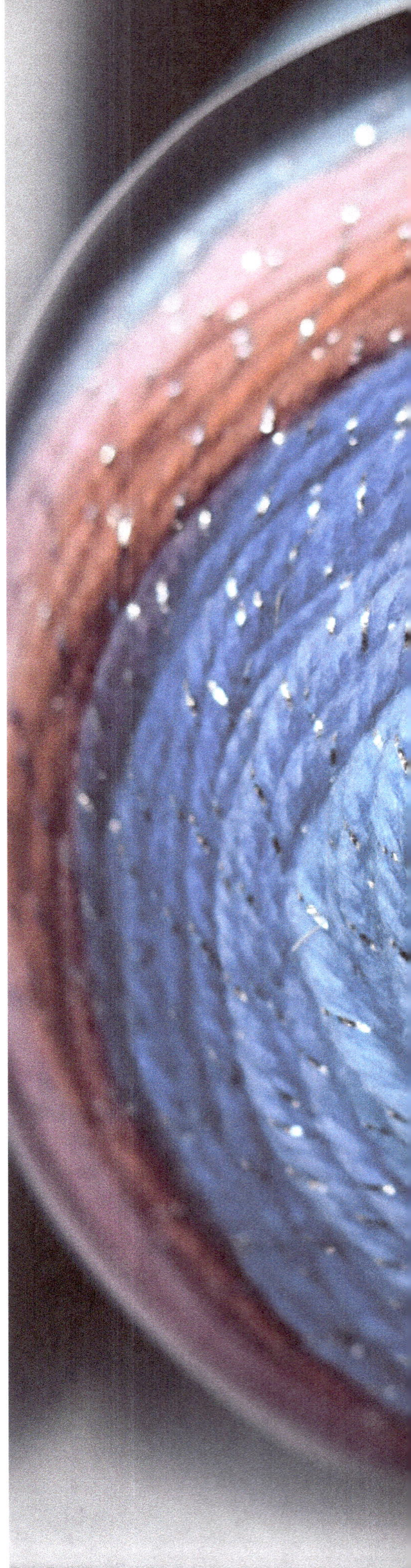

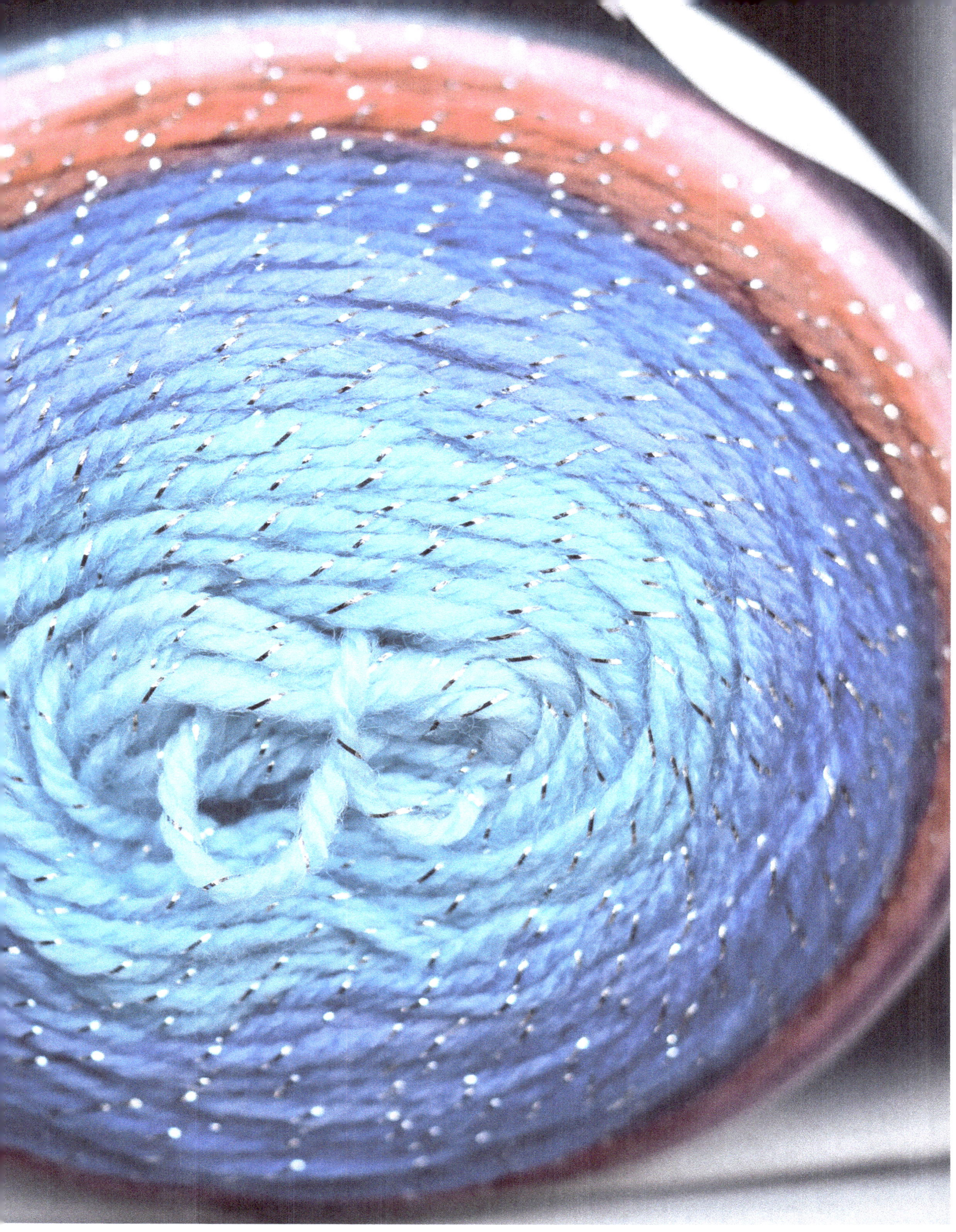

Conclusion

It is no longer news that digital die-cutting units are incredibly restrictive for craft enthusiasts and people who love the Cricut die-cutting system.

They mostly allow users to cut a small number of fonts, and they are not cheap at all.

Thankfully, a few programs out there have managed to open Cricut to enable them to cut designs, TrueType fonts created by users, and many more.

Below is a list of the best third-party software to use with Cricut.

Make the Cut

This is an excellent third-party Cricut Design software that comes with simple but highly effective design features, e.g. it packs quick lattice tools, and it can convert raster images into vectors for cutting. The program has been around for some time. Some of the most outstanding features of the tool include:

It comes with advanced editing tools, and it is relatively easy to use (even for a newbie) because the user interface is effortless to learn.

·The software works with many file formats, and it also uses TrueType fonts.

·The software comes with a pixel trace tool that allows users to take and convert raster graphics into vector paths for cutting.

For those that are interested, Make the Cut works with Gazelle, Craft ROBO, Wishblade, and Silhouette.

·Some other features include the fact that users can import the following: WPC, GSD, PS, AI9, EPS, OTF, TTF, SCUT, or PDF files and can also export shapes in SVG, Ai, EPS, PNG, and JPG formats.

Make the Cut is a user-friendly and flexible Cricut-related software that adds more utility to the digital die-cutting machine that is usually limited in usage and application.

Sure, Cuts A Lot

The Sure Cuts A Lot of software gives users complete control of their designs without the cartridges' restrictions featured in Cricut DesignStudio.

Users must install a firmware update to their Cricut die-cutting machine; however, they can do this for free by downloading the trial version of DesignStudio. It is a straightforward task to perform.

Some of the features of the Sure Cuts A Lot software include:

•It allows users to use the OpenType and TrueType fonts.

It is the one and only Cricut Design tool available that comes with freestyle drawing tools.

•It allows users to create unique designs with basic drawing and editing tools.

•The program works with Silhouette, Craft ROBO, and Wishblade die-cutting machines.

•It is specifically designed to open up all of Cricut's cutting features and abilities.

•It allows users to edit the individual nodes that make up the path.

•It comes with an auto trace feature that converts raster graphics into vector images.

•The programs have about 200 built-in shapes and other exciting features.

•It allows users to import different file formats, including PDF, SVG, AI, EPS, and WPC. The pro version allows users to import DXF and PLT.

•It allows users to select styles, including Blackout and Shadow, to quickly change shapes and letters with just a few clicks of the mouse.

•It allows users to use advanced features such as layers, grouping, and the weld tool to make the most out of their designs.

To download and get the complete set of Sure Cuts A Lot of features, you can check their website. The Sure Cuts A Lot program doesn't came with fonts; it only allows users to use the already on their computers.

Getting more fonts to your computer isn't a big deal because thousands of fonts are out there. Besides, you don't have to buy any special cartridges to get more fonts to your system.

Cricut DesignStudio

Cricut DesignStudio, a product of ProvoCraft, allows users to connect Cricut to a personal computer to do much more with Cricut fonts and shapes.

For those that don't know, Provo Craft is the same company that manu-factures Cricut die-cutting machines. With the aid of various tools, this Cricut software allows users to adjust fonts and shapes.

Some of the best features of the software include:

·Users will be able to weld, flip, and rotate easily.

Users have the option of previewing and creating designs with different images from the Cricut library.

·Users will have to purchase a cartridge to cut.

·The software comes with a high level of customization to the Cricut library, and the extra features are beneficial.

·People who use this software are still limited to the same shapes and fonts from the cartridges they own but bearing in mind the tools packed in the program, which is not an issue.

The program remains a perfect option to use alongside your Cricut, and you'll be able to get the best out of its features. To know more about the software, go to their official website.

Inkscape

Inkscape is an open-source graphics editor for Windows and other operating systems. It is a professional program that costs absolutely nothing.

Users can use the program and Cricut to create and edit vector graphics such as illustrations, diagrams, line arts, logos, elaborate paintings, and much more.

Below are some of the features that come with the software:

It can be used to render primitive text and vector shapes.

·It supports embedding and optional tracing of raster graphics.

·The objects can be filled with solid colors, patterns, radial, linear color gradients, and others; their borders can be stroked with adjustable transparency.

·The program can be used to create vector graphics from multiple raster sources and pictures.

·Shapes created can be manipulated easily with different transformations: moving, rotating, scaling, and skewing.

There are many more features present in this powerful software, and the easiest way to get acquainted with them all is to visit Inkscape's official website.

To maximize the use of your Cricut machine, you should consider using these excellent software applications that are compatible with Windows systems.

For the best experience possible, you should pair them up with some 2D digital pixel art tools or with some photo editors.

Depending on what you choose to do, you will quickly take control of your creativity and use Cricut Design Space the way you've always dreamt of.

Thank you !!

www.ingramcontent.com/pod-product-compliance
Lightning Source LLC
Chambersburg PA
CBHW080456030726
47592CB00011B/3143